Memorials Of The Family Of Forbes Of Forbesfield

Memorials of the Family of
Forbes of Forbesfield

With Notes on Connected
Morgans, Duncans and Fergusons

By
Alexander Forbes

Aberdeen
The King's Printers
1905

Forbes of Forbesfield

Only 150 copies printed.

No. /33

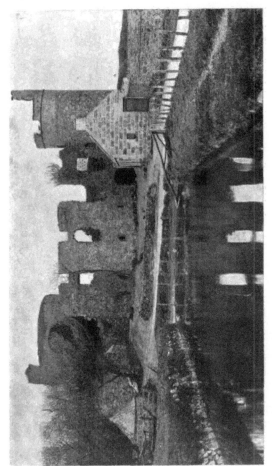

PITSLIGO CASTLE

Tower built about 1424 by Sir William, second son of Sir John Forbes of Druminnor

o

Memorials of the Family of

Forbes of Forbesfield

With Notes on Connected

Morgans, Duncans and Fergusons

By

Alexander Forbes

Aberdeen

The King's Printers

1905

To my Nephews.

At your request I have had put into literary form the facts contained in the following pages. They have been collected at considerable trouble, but I think I may say their accuracy may be relied upon.

I cannot exaggerate or adequately acknowledge my obligations to Mr. P. J. Anderson, Librarian of the University, and Mr. A. M. Munro, Assistant City Chamberlain, for the interest they have throughout taken in the subject, and the invaluable help they have given during its preparation, which has greatly lightened my labours and added to the value of the work.

Alexander Forbes.

1 Albyn Terrace,
    Aberdeen, November, 1904.

Contents

List of Illustrations

Forbes of Forbes

I. Duncan de Forbes

The first of the Family of Forbes of whom there is authentic record was Duncan de Forbes, who had a Charter by King Alexander III. of the lands of Forbes in 1272. "King Alexander gave and disponed to Duncan Forbeys tenementum de Forbeys, that is the lands and heretage of Forbeys quhilk charter is yet extant."[1]

The old evidents of the Lords Forbes were revised by Sir John Skene, His Majesty's Clerk Register, in the month of September, 1593, when he stated that Alexander III., in the 23rd year of his reign, which is the year of God 1272, gave and disponed to Duncan Lord Forbes terras et tenementum de Forbes.[2]

II. John de Forbes

whose lands were forfeited after the conquest of Scotland by the English in 1303, was probably son of the last—and Governor of the Castle of Urquhart. Reference to the forfeiture of John Forbes' lands is made in 1306 when competing claims were made for them by Robert Chival and William Comyn brother to Sir John Comyn.[3]

That he was Governor of the Castle of Urquhart rests on the tradition given by Boece, who states that after a brave resistance against King Edward, the castle was taken by storm and the inmates put to the sword, except the wife of Alexander Bois, the Governor, who escaped, and that she was delivered of a posthumous son of whom the Forbeses are descended. As to the origin of the name this account is at variance with fact, but if the story is otherwise correct the probability is that John de Forbes was the Governor and Sir Christian who appears to have

[1] Note by Sir John Skene in *De Verborum Significatione*.

[2] Antiquities of Aberdeen and Banff, IV. 372.

[3] Palgrave's Documents, &c., illustrating the History of Scotland, I. pp. 312, 314; Antiquities, IV. 373.

distinguished himself under King Robert, the son by whom the line of the family was preserved.

III. Sir Christian de Forbes

who had a charter from King Robert Bruce in 1325. A charter was granted by King Robert Bruce to Sir Christian de Forbes Knight of the third part of the davach of Ardach and of the third part of the davach of Skeeth in the barony of Deskford dated 27th March 1325.[1]

According to Boece, Forbes fell at Duplin in 1332 and the name was again preserved by a posthumous son. Sir Christian is not afterwards mentioned and probably did fall at Duplin, and the absence of the name in official documents issued at the period seems to indicate that few of the family returned from the fatal field.

IV. John de Forbes

In 1359 John de Forbes "dominus ejusdem" was witness to two charters granted by Thomas Earl of Mar.[2] He had charters of several lands by King David II. and King Robert II.

On 3rd July, 1364, David II. confirmed a charter by Thomas Earl of Mar to John de Forbes "dominus ejusdem" of the lands of Edinbanchory and Craglogy. He also had a charter of confirmation of the same lands 15th November, 1374.[3]

In the same year (1374) he was acting Sheriff of Aberdeen for Alexander Fraser of Philorth.[4] On 21st October, 1375, he was one of the two Procurators for the Bishop of Moray in the settlement of a claim by one of the Bishop's tenants.[5] He had a charter granted by the Bishop of Moray to himself and Margaret his wife of the lands of Fynrossy, on the Loch of Spynie, dated 18th July, 1378. In April, 1380, he appears as witness to the confirmation of a charter by Andrew of Leslie of the lands of Kinbruyn and Badechash in the barony of Rothienorman.[6]

1 Antiquities, IV. 760. 2 Antiquities, IV. 716, 717.

3 Antiquities, IV. 373, 374 ; Maitland Club Miscell. I. 378.

4 Exchequer Rolls, II. 426. 5 Reg. Epis. Morav. 180, 181. 6 Antiquities, III. 552.

He died before 20th August, 1387, and it is said "was a gude man wise mychty and manly in his tyme."[1] By his wife, Margaret, he had a son, JOHN, who suceeeded him.

V. Sir John de Forbes

married Elizabeth, daughter of Kennedy of Dunure, by whom he had four sons :—

> 1. Sir ALEXANDER, his heir. He was among the Scottish Forces sent to the assistance of Charles, Dauphin of France (afterwards King Charles VII.), and had a share in the victory obtained over the English at Bauge, in Anjou, 22nd March, 1421, in which the Duke of Clarence, commander of the hostile army, was killed. Soon after, at the desire of King James I. (then the prisoner of King Henry V.), he left the French service. He obtained a letter of safe conduct, dated at Dover, 9th June, 1421, to come by water into England, and remain there and go from thence ; also another dated 14th October, 1421, permitting Alexander Forbes, Knight, Lord of Forbes in Scotland, and forty men-at-arms with their attendants to the number of 100 persons or under, a safe conduct into England. He was shortly after 1436 created a Peer of Parliament. Alexander Lord Forbes died in 1448 ; he married Lady Elizabeth Douglas, only daughter of George Earl of Angus, granddaughter of Robert II., and their lineal descendant in the fourteenth generation now holds the title : Horace, 19th Lord Forbes.
>
> 2. Sir WILLIAM of Kynnaldy, of whom afterwards.
>
> 3. Sir JOHN of Tolquhon.
>
> 4. ALEXANDER of Brux—" Alister-Cam."

Lumsden states in his family history that he was called Sir John Forbes with the black lip by a mark he had on his face. He is first mentioned as Lord of Forbes 20th August, 1387, in the settlement of a dispute between him and Adam Bishop of Aberdeen regarding the

[1] Reg. Epis. Abd. I. 176, 238.

marches of the lands of Lurgyndaspok (Knockespok), when it was agreed that these lands which had been held in common between the Bishop and John of Forbes deceased should be in common between Forbes and the Bishop during the latter's incumbency. On the Bishop's death two years after, the dispute was renewed with his successor, and on 6th April, 1391, Robert III. granted a warrant to perambulate the marches of the lands. It was mutually agreed on 5th July following that the lands of Lurgyndaspok between the burns of Condeland and Cotburne from head to foot, and the lands of Tulycoscheny, should be in common between the Bishop of Aberdeen and Sir John Forbes, Knight, during their lifetime.[1]

In 1394 Sir John was appointed Justiciary and Coroner of Aberdeenshire.[2]

On 8th November, 1402, Sir John and his son, Alexander of Forbes, had charter by Isabel of Douglas Lady of Mar of the lands of Edinbanchory and Craglogy.[3]

On 2nd January, 1404-5, he paid to Alexander Stewart Earl of Mar, Sheriff Depute of Aberdeen, 40 merks of the issue of the court last held by the Duke of Albany.[4]

He was frequently a witness to charters up to May, 1406, and before 20th November of that year he was succeeded by his son.

1 Reg. Epis. Abd. I. 176, 187-189.   2 Crawford's Peerage, 146.
3 Antiquities, IV. 170.   4 Antiquities, IV. 457.

Forbes of Pitsligo

I. Sir William Forbes of Kynnaldy

2nd son of Sir John Forbes of Forbes, married in 1423 Agnes, only daughter of Sir William Fraser of Philorth, and by her he had at least two sons :—

1. ALEXANDER, his heir.
2. MALCOLM, of Mekil Wardris.

Sir William acquired from his brother Alexander, first Lord Forbes, the lands of Kynnaldy, Gordy, Davach, Manach and Petnamone, in the parish of Coldstone, County of Aberdeen, of which he had a charter by the Superior, Alexander Stewart Earl of Mar, dated " apud Aberdeen in festo Sancti Bartholomei 1419."

He acquired, by his marriage with Agnes Fraser, the lands of Glaslach, Coulcanock, Tulynamolt, Nether Bulgny, Mydelmaste, Over Bulgne, Achlin with the Mill of Bulgne and the stone quarry of Culburty in the barony of Aberdour and County of Aberdeen. The charter granted by James Douglas, Lord of Balveny and overlord of Aberdour, is dated at Falkland, 24th July, 1423.[1]

He had also a charter of these lands together with the adjoining lands of Petslegach and Achmacludy, dated 12th August, 1424, which charter was confirmed by James I., 18th July, 1426. On 6th November, 1423, he was infeft by John, Earl of Buchan, in the lands of Carnywhinge, Brekor-Vor and Litil Brekor, in the barony of Kin-Edwarte.[2] On 27th July, 1429, he had a charter by King James I., erecting the lands of Kynnaldy, Gordy, Davach, Manach, Petnamone, and Knocksoul into a free barony, in which charter he is styled William of Forbes, Knight.[3]

Sir William had a charter by Alexander of Setoun Lord of Gordon of the lands of Mekyl Wardris in the Garioch, dated 29th June, 1432, and on 21st June, 1433, he had a charter by Robert of Erskine of the

---

1 Crawford's Lives of the Officers of State in Scotland, p. 280; Antiquities, II. 380.

2 Antiquities, III. 521.   3 Reg. Mag. Sig.

lands of Laskgoune in the parish of Slains.[1]   He sold these lands to Gilbert Menzies, burgess of Aberdeen, on 3rd November, 1435. On 10th July, 1439, Sir William Forbes granted a bond on the same lands to Gilbert Menzies for the sum of sixty-eight pounds, and in 1473 John Menzies, son and heir of James Menzies of Laskgoune, sold to his uncle, Alexander Menzies, burgess of Aberdeen, a half third part of the lands of Laskgoune for a certain sum of money which had been paid by the said Alexander to John's uncle, Arthur Forbes, in discharge of a debt owing to his father, the said James Menzies.

It would appear from the transactions connected with Laskgoune that Sir William Forbes of Kynnaldy and Pitsligo had a son—

3. ARTHUR, married to Beatrice Countess of Errol (whose first husband, William, 1st Earl of Errol, died 19th August, 1460); and

4. A daughter married to James Menzies of Laskgoune, probably son of Gilbert, to whom Sir William sold the lands in 1435. Neither of these connections is referred to in Lumsden's Genealogy.

In 1444 (the precise date is not given), Sir William had a gift from King James II. of the lands of Bochrom and Kyninmont in the County of Banff during his lifetime.[2]

He died 23rd January, 1445, and was succeeded by his eldest son.

II. Sir Alexander Forbes

of Pitsligo, Knight, married Maria, daughter of the Earl of Errol,[3] by whom he had three sons and several daughters :—

1. WILLIAM, his heir apparent, married Mariot, daughter of Sir John Ogilvy of Lintrathan by whom he had two sons—

    (1). ALEXANDER, his heir, and

    (2). WILLIAM of Daach, of whom afterwards.

2. GEORGE of Lethendy.

3. ARTHUR of Rires.

4. One daughter married to John Gordon of Botary.

5. One to Alexander Urquhart, Sheriff of Cromarty.

6. One to Alexander Tulloch of Montcoffer.

7. One to Mowat of Balquholly.

8. One to Gilbert de Johnston of Caskieben.

1 Collections, I. 556.   2 Exchequer Rolls, V. 170.   3 Donean Tourist, p. 59.

ALEXANDER 4th LORD FORBES OF PITSLIGO

1678 -1762

Was out in the Rebellion, 1715 and 1745

Forbes of Pitsligo

Sir Alexander died in March, 1477, and his eldest son, William, having predeceased him, he was succeeded by his grandson, Alexander III. of Pitsligo. His great-great-great-grandson, Alexander VIII. of Pitsligo, was on 24th June, 1633, created Lord Forbes of Pitsligo in the Peerage of Scotland, with remainder to heirs male of his body or their heirs, whom failing to his heirs male whomsoever of the name of Forbes. Alexander fourth Lord Forbes of Pitsligo was attainted in 1746 by an Act of Parliament, in which he was wrongly described as Lord Pitsligo; but the House of Lords upheld the attainder. His only son John died without issue in 1781, and in his person the heirs male of the body of Alexander first Lord Forbes of Pitsligo became extinct.[1] A claim to the dignity was prepared by the late Mr. Cosmo Innes on behalf of the heir general of the heir male of the body of the grantee, Sir John Stuart Forbes, eighth baronet of Monymusk, whose great-grandfather, the fifth baronet, was son and heir of John Forbes (son of the fourth baronet) by Mary, daughter of Alexander, third Lord Forbes of Pitsligo.[2] The death of Sir J. S. Forbes in 1866 stopped further proceedings.[3]

1 Hewlett's Scotch Dignities, p. 143.   2 G. E. C.'s Complete Baronetage, p. 305.
3 See Appendix R.

Forbes of Newe

William Forbes of Daach

William Forbes, 2nd son of William Forbes, younger of Pitsligo, is designed of Daach. He married Elizabeth, daughter of John Forbes of Brux, called from his fair complexion the "White Laird," by whom he had two sons :—

1. ALEXANDER of Newe.
2. JOHN of Sunhonny.

He died about 1500, and was succeeded by his eldest son.

I. Alexander Forbes of Newe

He married Jean, daughter of Robert Lumsden of Medlar, afterwards of Cushnie, by whom he had two sons and several daughters :—

1. WILLIAM, his heir.
2. PATRICK of Pitellachie.
3. ISABEL, married 1st to Robert Coutts of Auchtercoull and had issue. Married 2nd to James Farquharson, and 3rd to Robert Middleton.
4. MARGARET, married 1st to William Skene of Auchtererne, and 2nd to Arthur Skene.[1]
5. Another daughter married to Robert Ross of Birsemoir.

He died in 1561 at Auchtercoull, and was succeeded by his eldest son.

II. William Forbes

Married Margaret, daughter of John Gordon of Botarie, by whom he had three sons and several daughters :—

1. JOHN, his heir.
2. ALEXANDER of Invernochty.
3. JAMES of Easter Migvie.

[1] Family MS. ; Skene Memorials.

8

William Forbes had charter of Newe[1] from Robert Lord Elphinstone, dated at Elphinstone 10th May, 1560, and had sasine of the lands and mill 14th July, 1560.

He died in 1571, and was interred in the Church of Strathdon. He was succeeded by his eldest son.

III. John Forbes

Married Isobel, daughter of Burnet of Leys, by whom he had three sons and two daughters :—

1. ALEXANDER, his heir.
2. ARTHUR of Culquhanny.
3. JOHN, called " Blind John."
4. MARJORY, married to William Leith of Newlands, to whom she had a daughter Isobel, who on 22nd November, 1645, obtained by a jury at Aberdeen a certificate of her descent.[2]
5. Another daughter died young.

John Forbes had sasine from Lord Elphinstone as heir to his father, William Forbes, dated 27th August, 1572, and charter from Alexander, Master of Elphinstone, to him and his heirs male, dated 23rd May, 1591. John Forbes granted charter of Newe, &c. to his son, Alexander, dated 25th June, 1612 ; and Alexander Forbes had sasine from Alexander Lord Elphinstone as heir to his father, John Forbes, dated 2nd December, 1616. He was called " Blue Bonnet,"[3] and built the mansion house of Newe in 1604—it forms part of the present Castle, still shewing the original motto, " Justitia Columna Domus."

He died in Aberdeen 28th January, 1616, and was interred there. He was succeeded by his eldest son.

IV. Alexander Forbes

Married Janet, daughter of Robertson of Lude in Atholl, by whom he had two sons and three daughters :—

1. WILLIAM, his heir.
2. JOHN of Newlands. He probably married his cousin, Isobel Leith, and by her acquired the property of Newlands.

1 Newe Titles.   2 Miscell. Spalding Club, V. 328.   3 Family MS.

3. ISOBEL, married to William Forbes of Skellater, 11th July, 1675.[1]

4. ——— married to —— Gordon of Blelack.

5. ——— married to Donald Cattanach of Tolquhill.

Alexander Forbes had sasine of the lands on 10th April, 1627, proceeding on charter granted him by John Earl of Mar, dated 17th September, 1626.

He died 14th November, 1654, and was interred in the Church of Strathdon. He was succeeded by his eldest son.

V. William Forbes

Married Helen, daughter of Arthur Forbes of Culquhanny, his cousin, by whom he had four sons and four daughters[2] :—

1. WILLIAM, his heir.

2. PATRICK, merchant in Aberdeen, and had one son who died without succession. Patrick Forbes had sasine of the lands of Mill of Newe and that portion sold by Arthur Forbes of Culquhanny, 16th May, 1670, proceeding on a disposition of these lands by the said William Forbes to the said Patrick Forbes, dated 14th February, 1670.

3. GEORGE of Bellabeg, baptised 10th June, 1668, married 4th September, 1701, Isobel Forbes, daughter of deceased William Forbes of Asloun. His grandson, John Forbes, Bombay, purchased the estate of Newe, 12th September, 1792, from James Forbes of Seaton (see p. 12). Charles Forbes of Newe, nephew and heir of John Forbes, Bombay, was created a baronet of the United Kingdom, 4th November, 1823; and was, in error,[3] served heir male general to his great-grandfather, William Forbes V. of Newe, on 12th March, 1830; to his ancestor William Forbes of Daach, on 4th October, 1830; and to his cousin Alexander, third Lord Forbes of Pitsligo, on 12th January, 1833.

4. JOHN of Deskrie, married, 22nd August, 1699, to Margaret Farquharson of Belenach.

5. ISOBEL, married, 7th July, 1675, to George Forbes of Skellater.

1 Par. Register.   2 Strathdon Parish Registers.   3 See Appendix M.

6. MARJORIE, married, 24th December, 1693, to Francis Couper, in Cemcile.

7. HELEN, married, 6th December, 1687, Adam Panton, in the Parish of Belhelvie, and had issue.

8. AGNES, baptised 16th September, 1674; married, 19th August, 1697, to William Forbes of Belnabodach.

William Forbes, son and heir of Alexander Forbes, had sasine of the lands on 2nd December, 1657, proceeding on precept, granted by John Earl of Mar, in his favour, 5th November, 1657. There was a contract of marches between William Forbes of Newe and John Forbes of Buchaam, dated 20th July, 1669.

William Forbes, fifth of Newe, died 10th January, 1698, and was interred in the Church of Strathdon. He was succeeded by his eldest son.

VI. William Forbes

Married, first, 12th September, 1678, Christian, 3rd daughter of Alexander Forbes of Boyndlie, by whom he had one daughter—

JEAN, baptised 29th June, 1682; she married Nathaniel Forbes of Ardgeith.

He married, secondly, Isobel, daughter of Thomas Stewart of Drumin, by whom he had issue[1] :—

1. JOHN, his heir, baptised 9th December, 1686; married, 3rd July, 1707, Sophia, daughter of deceased Arthur Forbes of Brux.

2. ALEXANDER, baptised 22nd December, 1687, from whom are descended the family of the late Baillie James Forbes of Aberdeen, who therefore are now the representatives of the Forbeses of Daach and Newe, and the heirs male general of the Lords Forbes of Pitsligo.

3. WILLIAM, baptised 22nd January, 1689; died without succession in his 20th year.

4. JEAN, baptised 29th June, 1682; married, 3rd July, 1701, Nathaniel Forbes of Ripachie.

5. HELEN, baptised 3rd September, 1685.

1 Strathdon Registers.

6. ISOBEL, baptised 9th March, 1693; married to John Shaw in Glencarvie.
7. ANNA, baptised   October, 1694, married to Alexander Michie in Buchaam.
8. ELSPET, baptised 12th June, 1696.

William Forbes, sixth of Newe, died 22nd July, 1699, and was succeeded by his son, John, whose grandson John, ninth laird, sold the estate of Newe, 18th November, 1779, to James Forbes of Seaton; and, dying on 1st February, 1792, terminated the direct male line of the family; but an only daughter, Mary, married Sir Archibald Grant, fourth baronet of Monymusk.

forbes in New Balgonen

Alexander Forbes

Alexander Forbes, second son of William Forbes, sixth of Newe, baptised there 22nd December, 1687, had the farm of New Balgonen, Keig (now called Airlie). He married Margaret, daughter of Alexander Gellan, in Bithney, Parish of Forbes, by his wife, Margaret Morgan. Alexander Forbes died 4th August, 1740, in his 53rd year, and was interred in the Old Churchyard of Forbes, where a stone records the fact (see Appendix A.). His spouse died 30th November, 1752, in Aberdeen, and was interred in Saint Nicholas Churchyard. Issue :—

Alexander, Francis, John, Samuel, Robert, Joseph, Ann, Margaret—Alexander and Ann died in infancy. (The Schoolhouse at Keig was at one time burned, with all the Parish Registers, hence the impossibility of procuring the dates of birth).[1]

2. FRANCIS, the second son, was a writer in Aberdeen, and collector of land and other taxes for the City and County. Elected a Burgess of Guild, 28th August, 1766. He married, first, Ann, daughter of James Ellis, 18th June, 1759, by whom he had a daughter,

    (1). MARGARET, baptised 19th April, 1760, by Rev. Mr. Riddoch, St. Paul's. She married Robert Luckie, manufacturer in Aberdeen, and died without issue. Her mother, Ann Ellis, died 6th May, 1760.

Francis Forbes married, secondly, Elizabeth, daughter of James Fraser, on 11th January, 1762, by whom he had issue :—

    (1). FRANCIS, baptised 29th June, 1766, died 1767.
    (2). ELIZABETH, baptised 8th September, 1763, died 1766.
    (3). JEAN, baptised 25th April, 1765, died 1769.

1 New Spalding Club Miscellany, I., 196.

13

    (4). ELIZABETH, baptised 11th October, 1768, died 1769.

Francis Forbes died 13th May, 1769. Elizabeth Fraser, his relict, died 22nd May, 1769. They were both buried in St. Nicholas Churchyard.

    On 10th June, 1769, Betty Forbes was served heir general to her mother, Betty Fraser, wife of Francis Forbes, writer. On 11th November, 1769, Margaret Forbes was served heir general to her sister, Betty, daughter of Francis Forbes, writer.

3. JOHN, third son of Alexander Forbes in New Balgonen, of whom afterwards.

4. SAMUEL, fourth son of Alexander Forbes in New Balgonen, had the farm of Old Flinders, Kennethmont. He married Jean Johnston, and had issue :—

    (1). SAMUEL, farmer in Westfield, Kennethmont. He married Janet Scott, and had issue :—
        i. SAMUEL.
        ii. WILLIAM.
        iii. MARY.
        iv. JESSY.
        v. ANN.

    (2). ROBERT, farmer in Flinders, Kennethmont. Married and had issue :—
        i. ROBERT, farmer in Old Flinders. Married, 1864, Ann Grant, and had issue :—
            (i). JESSY ANN, born 1868.
            (ii). MARY JANE, born 1870.
            (iii). CHRISTINA THOMSON, born 1873.
            (iv). GEORGINA JOHNSTON, born 1875.
        ii. JOHN, farmer in Flinders. Married Christina Thomson, and had issue :—
            (i). One daughter, CHRISTINA, born 1863.
        iii. JESSY.

    (3). MARGARET.

    (4). ANN.

5. ROBERT, fifth son of Alexander Forbes in New Balgonen, went to Tobago in the West Indies as an overseer of blacks, but his health failing he returned home, and died at Old Flinders, in 1764, unmarried. He was buried in St. Nicholas Churchyard, 4th January, 1764.

6. JOSEPH, sixth son of Alexander Forbes in New Balgonen, admitted a Freeman of the Wright and Cooper Incorporation on 30th April, 1751. There were contracted in order to marriage on 1st April, 1751, Joseph Forbes, cabinetmaker in Aberdeen, and Margaret Christall, lawful daughter of the deceased Convener, William Christall there. Cautioners William Forbes, merchant, and Provost Aberdein. Paid for the poor £8. A numerous family were the issue of this marriage, but they nearly all died in infancy :—

    (1). A SON, baptised 3rd February, 1752. Entry in register incomplete — probably Alexander, after the grandfather.

    (2). WILLIAM, baptised 14th September, 1753.

    (3). JOSEPH, baptised 29th June, 1758, in presence of John Burnet, Campfield.

    (4). GEORGE, baptised 18th April, 1762, by Professor Gerard, D.D.

    (5). HUGH, baptised 29th March, 1764, in presence of Algernon Johnston, merchant, and William Mitchell.

    (6). BENJAMIN, baptised 21st October, 1765, by Rev. Mr. Innes, in presence of George Forbes and William Forbes.

    (7). WILLIAM, baptised 23rd April, 1769, by Rev. Mr. Innes, in presence of William Forbes, merchant, and George Forbes of Ledmacoy.

    (8). MARGARET, baptised 1st March, 1755.

    (9). ELIZABETH, baptised 26th June, 1756.

    (10). JEAN, baptised 28th August, 1760.

(11). ANN, baptised 9th May, 1767, by Rev. Mr. Innes, Episcopal Minister, in presence of Ninian Johnston and William Forbes, merchants.

Joseph Forbes died 18th December, 1799. Margaret Christall, his spouse, died 28th October, 1777. Both were interred in St. Nicholas Churchyard. Joseph Forbes may have married a a second wife, although no record exists to that effect so far as I can discover, but a Mrs. Joseph Forbes is recorded to have been interred in Aberdeen on 2nd January, 1800. She may have been a son's wife.[1]

8. MARGARET, daughter of Alexander Forbes in New Balgonen, married John Johnston in Old Flinders, Kennethmont, and had issue.

After the death of Alexander Forbes in 1740, the widow, it is recorded, being well left, removed to Aberdeen for the better education of her family.[2]

[1] St. Nicholas Parish Registers.

[2] Letters of James Smith, Tullynessle, dated 29th May and 8th June, 1850.

BONNYMUIR

FORBESFIELD

Forbes of Forbesfield

I. John Forbes

JOHN, third son of Alexander Forbes in New Balgonen, was educated partly in the country and afterwards in Aberdeen. Admitted Burgess of Trade, 27th August, 1761. Acquired, about 1773, the property of Forbesfield, near Aberdeen. In addition to his business, he acted largely as a banker, and at his death in 1785, the inventory of his effects contained many bills on gentlemen in the city and county for considerable amounts ; these bills were mostly granted for six and twelve months, and the rate of interest charged was invariably five per cent. per annum. Among them were several bills granted by his kinsmen, Alexander and John Forbes of Inverernan. His inventory also contained a considerable quantity of silver plate and many books chiefly of a religious character. He was an elder in the Established Church, and, judging from letters still extant received at the time of his death, must have been greatly and generally esteemed for his upright character and kindly disposition and benevolence.

He married, August, 1763, Anne, daughter of Alexander Ferguson (of the family of Badifurrow, now Manar, afterwards of Pitfour and Kinmundy), merchant in Aberdeen, afterwards Baillie in Inverurie and Town Clerk there, in succession to his father-in-law, George Scott ; and had issue :—

    1. ALEXANDER, baptised 19th December, 1765, by Rev. Mr. Ogilvie, in presence of James Black, merchant, and Francis Forbes, writer.

    2. JOHN, baptised 7th July, 1768, by Rev. Mr. Ogilvie, in presence of Francis Forbes, writer, and James Black, merchant. He died 22nd June, 1773.

    3. JOHN, baptised 20th May, 1774, by Rev. Thomas Forbes, in presence of James Black, Senior, and Andrew Tait, organist.

17

4. ROBERT, baptised 7th November, 1775, by Rev. Thomas Forbes, in presence of James Black, Senior, and David Morice, writer in Aberdeen. He died 9th September, 1779.
5. JAMES, baptised 4th July, 1777, by Rev. Mr. Abercrombie, in presence of John Forbes, Junior, Invererman, and James Ferguson, Esq. of Kinmundy.
6. ROBERT, baptised 27th April, 1780, by Rev. Mr. James Sherriff, in presence of Mr. David Morice, Junior, advocate, and John Leslie, Junior, goldsmith, both in Aberdeen.
7. MARGARET, baptised 17th September, 1764, by Rev. Mr. Ogilvie, in presence of Alexander Ferguson, writer, Edinburgh, and Francis Forbes, writer, Aberdeen.
8. MARY, baptised 15th May, 1770, by Rev. Mr. Ogilvie, in presence of James Black, merchant.
9. CHRISTIAN, baptised 3rd October, 1772, by Rev. Mr. Forbes, in presence of James Black, Senior, and James Black, Junior, his son.

Of this family of nine, only four grew up, viz. :—

3. JOHN, baptised 1774; educated at the Grammar School and at Marischal College and University, 1788-90. He purposed to follow the Law, and on 13th July, 1790, dues were paid by him to the Society of Procurators in Aberdeen, £1.1.0; and on 15th January, 1791, he paid for apprentice fee to David Morice, advocate, £16.13.4. He, however, did not prosecute the Law. On 2nd July, 1795, he joined as Ensign the Aberdeen Volunteers, when a uniform was got for him value £8 sterling. He purchased 25th August, 1798, a commission in the 53rd Foot, and was promoted to be Lieutenant, 5th December, 1799, but resigned his commission, 10th July, 1801. He never appears to have joined his regiment, which was at that time stationed at St. Lucia in the West Indies. It was not an uncommon thing at this time for a man having influence to obtain a commission long before he really intended to join his regiment, the object being to acquire seniority, and the same influence was necessary to obtain continous leave of absence. He died abroad subsequent to 1802— unmarried.[1]

1 Letter from Public Record Office, London.

JAMES FORBES OF FORBESFIELD
1777—1834

Lieutenant ROBERT FORBES
1780—1804

5. JAMES, of whom afterwards.
6. ROBERT, third surviving son of John Forbes of Forbesfield, baptised 27th April, 1780. Educated at the Grammar School and at Marischal College and University, 1793-94. Lieutenant H. E. I. C. S., Madras Presidency; died in India, 27th October, 1804, unmarried.[1]
8. MARY, baptised 15th May, 1770; married, 1798, John Machattie, ironfounder, Aberdeen, and had issue.

II. James Forbes

JAMES, second surviving son of John Forbes of Forbesfield. Baptised 4th July, 1777. Educated at the Grammar School, from which he went into the wholesale cloth business of Robert Lamb, whom he succeeded, and carried on a large business all over the North of Scotland in partnership with Mr. Johnston, under the firm of Johnston & Forbes. Mr. Johnston retired in 1823, when the style of the firm became James Forbes & Son until his death in 1834, when his son James took into partnership his brothers, John and Alexander, and the style of the firm became James Forbes & Sons. It has so remained into the 20th century and is still carried on by my brother James and myself, but the sphere of the firm's operations is no longer confined to the North of Scotland, the principal business now being done in England and the Colonies.

He joined the corps of Aberdeen Volunteers, 400 rank and file, formed in 1803 for the defence of the country against the threatened invasion by Napoleon : James Forbes, Gent., to be Ensign, gazetted 3rd November, 1804. He appears to have been subsequently gazetted 9th September, 1808: Ensign James Forbes to be Lieutenant in Aberdeenshire Militia, vice Jessiman resigned.[2] He joined the Guildry, 8th February, 1810, and was by ballot elected a member of the select committee appointed by the Burgesses of Guild, 15th February, 1817, to protect their interests against the mismanagement of their funds by the Town Council, and on 20th September of the same year he was again elected a member of a special committee for the same purpose.[3] He took a warm

1 Dodwell & Miles' List of Indian Officers, 1760 to 1834.

2 "Aberdeen Journal."   3 Kennedy's Annals of Aberdeen, I., pp. 358 and 368.

interest in the Narrow Wynd Friendly Society, was for some years their President, and received a silver snuff box on two occasions in acknowledgment of the services he had rendered the Society.

He married, in 1798, Elizabeth Fraser, of an Inverness-shire family, and had issue, who grew up :—

1. JAMES, born 15th July, 1800, of whom afterwards.

2. ROBERT, born 1803, joined in early life a Dragoon regiment, which he relinquished to become a schoolmaster in Aberdeenshire and afterwards in Edinburgh. He married in 1841, Mary Wildgoose, by whom he had issue :—

    (1.) ALEXANDER, who was in a cavalry regiment and in action at Majuba Hill, South Africa. He afterwards died of cholera in Egypt in 1882.

    (2.) HARRY LEITH LUMSDEN, teacher in a school in New York.

    (3.) MARY, for forty years one of the head teachers in Sharp's Educational Institute, Perth.

    Robert Forbes died at Edinburgh in 1851. His wife died there 31st January, 1879.

3. JOHN, born 4th July, 1807, was a merchant in Aberdeen and associated with his brothers in business. He died unmarried, 22nd August, 1834, and was interred in St. Nicholas Churchyard.

4. ALEXANDER, born 19th April, 1814, was educated at Ledingham's Academy and afterwards at Udny Academy under Dr. Bisset. He was associated with his brother James in business until 1860, when he commenced an independent business on his own account in Aberdeen, retiring in 1880. He resided at Morkeu, Cults, a property which he purchased in 1874. He was very fond of flowers, a taste he inherited from his father, which he cultivated there with great success. He paid a visit to India in 1883, and died 6th September, 1893, unmarried. He is interred in St. Nicholas Churchyard.

    By his will he left property to the amount of some £60,000— £4350 to be given in bequests to forty-one local charities, and the interest of one half of the residue among such deserving

indigent Burgesses of Guild of the city of Aberdeen, or widows
or daughters of deceased Burgesses, in such sums as his trustees
may fix—not less than £10 nor more than £15 yearly.   The
other half of the residue among such deserving indigent widows
or daughters who had seen better days, of deceased merchants,
shopkeepers, or other men of business who had resided in Aberdeen for at least 25 years, in such sums as his trustees may
fix—not less than £10 yearly.

5. ELIZABETH, born 1799; married, 31st March, 1819, Alexander
Taylor, merchant in Aberdeen, by whom she had

(1). FRANCIS TAYLOR,⎫ Both joined their father in business, and
(2). JAMES TAYLOR, ⎰   died at comparatively early ages.

(3). JOHN TAYLOR, lost at sea, 1842, on his first voyage, off a
barque called the "Prince of Wales."

(4). ANNE JOPP TAYLOR, born 1824; died, unmarried, 1903.

(5). JANE FORBES TAYLOR, born 1829.

(6). JOHANNA TAYLOR, born 1832; died, unmarried, December, 1901.

Alexander Taylor died in 1867, and his wife died in 1876.

6. JANE LE GRAND, born 1805; died, unmarried, 23rd December,
1879.

7. ANNE, born 1809; married, first, 1838, Rev. Alexander Gardiner,
minister of the Presbyterian Church, Fergus, Upper Canada, by
whom she had two daughters :—

(1). ANNE FORBES GARDINER, born at Fergus on 30th July,
1839, married, and has family.

(2). ELSIE ELIZA GARDINER, born 27th March, 1841, married,
3rd February, 1874, Alexander Dewar, St. Andrews,
Canada, and had issue, one daughter—

i. ANNIE FORBES DEWAR, born 12th April, 1876.

Mrs. Dewar died 25th July, 1885.

Their mother married for her second husband, 1856, Rev.
Alexander Sim, a Congregational minister in Canada, without
issue.   She died 3rd October, 1862.

21

8. SOPHIA ROBERTSON, born 1811; died, unmarried, 1876; interred in St. Nicholas Churchyard.

James Forbes sold Forbesfield, in 1811, to Duncan Davidson, advocate in Aberdeen. He died 24th May, 1834, and was buried in the family vault in St. Nicholas Churchyard. His wife died on 30th December, 1818, and was also buried there.

III. James Forbes

JAMES, eldest son of James Forbes, second of Forbesfield, born 15th July, 1800, was educated at the Grammar School and at Marischal College and University, where he graduated M.A. in 1818. From the Grammar School on two consecutive occasions he gained the first bursary, but did not accept. He studied Law for a short time in Edinburgh with the view of going to the Bar, but this he relinquished at the urgent request of his father to join him in his business in Aberdeen. Very early in life he developed a great capacity for public work, and soon took an active part in burgh and general politics. In 1824 he showed great gallantry in organising the students of Marischal College and inducing them to exercise their right by taking the election of their Lord Rector into their own hands, which had hitherto been appropriated by the professors appointing creatures of their own choice, and absentees who took no interest whatever in the students. A letter which he addressed to them had the desired effect; in it he said, " Elect no one who is related in any degree to a Peer or Baronet; for believe us, whatever he may tell you he is looking to his own interests at your expense, and will be happy to honour his relative by voting him Lord Rector. Elect none of those quiet, deceitful caterpillars who look on the constituted authorities as infallible, and who would lick the very dust beneath his feet to gain the favour of a professor. But elect bold, decisive fellows who speak what they think, and will not be intimidated."[1] This pamphlet had its desired effect, and Joseph Hume, M.P. was elected in 1824 and 1825 by 44 votes over the sitting Rector, the Earl of Fife, having a majority in all the

[1] Aberdeen Rectorial Addresses, page 33.

BAILLIE JAMES FORBES

1800—1870

nations. There had been no Rectorial Court held since 1738. Mr. Hume resuscitated them in 1825, very much to the disgust of the professors.[1]

He was elected to the Town Council in November, 1837, was appointed a Magistrate in 1839, but retired in consequence of the state of his health in 1846. On every occasion when he went to the poll, as proof of his immense popularity, he was returned at the top by larger numbers than other candidates in any of the municipal wards. He continued throughout life to take an active and leading part in almost every department of public life in Aberdeen. He was President of the Narrow Wynd Society instituted in 1660, an old friendly society for the benefit of its members, which, having outlived its day, was wound up under his auspices in 1867, on which occasion the few surviving members presented him with an elegant silver claret jug bearing a suitable inscription in token of their regard for him. He was Chairman of the first Parochial Board after the passing of the Act, and laid the foundation stone of St. Nicholas Poorhouse, 22nd April, 1848, with great ceremony. It was the earliest building for housing of the poor erected in Scotland.[2] He was promoter and Chairman of the City Public Baths; the founder, in 1852, of the North of Scotland Trade Protection Society, which afterwards became the Aberdeen Chamber of Commerce (incorporated), and continued, with exception of 12 months, President till his death. He was an original member of the Spalding Club, founded in 1839.

He took a keen interest in Imperial politics, first as a Tory acting on the committee of Provost James Hadden when he contested the city in opposition to Mr. Alexander Bannerman, in 1832, after the passing of the Reform Act; and again acting on the committee of Sir Arthur Farquhar, R.N., in 1835, who was unsuccessful in unseating Mr. Bannerman. From 1841 till his death in 1870 no conservative candidate came forward to contest Aberdeen, and when Mr. Bannerman retired, on his appointment as Governor of Prince Edward Island, he supported the candidature of Captain Alexander Dingwall Fordyce, R.N., a moderate Whig, acting as chairman of his election committee; in which capacity he continued to act for the successive Members of Parliament for Aberdeen, viz. :—Mr. George Thompson of Pitmedden and Colonel Sykes. He was

1 Aberdeen Rectorial Addresses, pp. 33 & 349. 2 "Aberdeen Journal," 26th April, 1848.

placed on the Commission of the Peace for the County of Aberdeen, 15th November, 1853, frequently taking his seat on the bench, and assisting the Naval Assessors in their enquiries into the causes of loss of life through shipwreck.

He took throughout life a very prominent part in university matters and all that concerned his Alma Mater, and took a leading part in endeavouring to prevent the fusion of the two colleges, but was in favour of a fusion of the two universities, giving at great length evidence before the Royal Commissioners when they sat in Aberdeen to enquire into the question in 1857, and recommending many of the beneficial changes that have been introduced in recent years (see Appendix P). After the Union was effected in 1860, he proved a zealous member of the General Council, then constituted, acting on its Business Committee till his death.

For many years he was chairman of the Local Marine Board. Became a Burgess of Guild, 16th September, 1831, and took a great interest in the affairs of the Guildry, and a prominent part on several occasions in endeavouring to obtain the right to the management of their own funds, receiving the thanks of the body for his valued services.

In 1863 he delivered a paper on the "Social Condition of Scotland during the fifteenth and sixteenth centuries" before the Social Science Association, which, on the motion of the chairman, it was unanimously resolved should be published by the Association; it went through several editions. It would be impossible even to indicate the valuable services which he rendered to his fellow-citizens of all classes in almost every capacity, for which reference must be made to the public prints of the day; and as he was certainly one of the ablest, he was at the same time the most respected and trusted and influential of the public men of his generation.

He married, on 15th April, 1828, Elspet Gordon, elder daughter of James Morgan of Bonnymuir—for many years a Planter in Jamaica—by Agnes Duncan, daughter of Robert Duncan, merchant, a prominent citizen and member of Town Council; by whom he had issue.

James Forbes died 29th December, 1870. His wife died 3rd May, 1856; both were interred in St. Nicholas Churchyard.

ELSPET GORDON MORGAN FORBES
1805—1856

JAMES FORBES

ALEXANDER FORBES

The Family of James Forbes and Elspet Gordon Morgan

1. JAMES, born 19th January, 1829, died 28th October, 1829.

2. JAMES, born 4th February, 1830. No incidents of much interest
   occurred to him during either boyhood or youth; he was
   a great reader and a good scholar, carrying off many prizes at
   Meston's and the Grammar School under Dr. Melvin. In 1843,
   he entered Marischal College and University, having gained a
   bursary of £5 value, which in these days, like all bursaries of
   whatever amount, was sufficient to meet all the fees and leave
   something over. He attended the University for three years but
   did not graduate. He entered his father's business in 1846.

   Being very fond of pedestrian excursions, he travelled over
   a considerable part of Scotland while quite young, along with his
   college classfellow, Dr. Archibald Simpson.

   He is very greatly interested in art and architecture, to
   which he has devoted much attention, and is a connoisseur of
   considerable taste. He is well informed in questions of public
   discussion, but has taken no active part in them outside the
   family circle. He is of a most equable temperament, and a
   great peacemaker on all occasions.

3. ALEXANDER (the author of these pages) was born in Kingsland
   House, Aberdeen, 9th June, 1835; educated at the Town's Public
   Schools and the Grammar School, entered his father's business
   in 1850, afterwards completing his business training in Man-
   chester. He returned to Aberdeen and joined in partnership his
   father and brother in the firm of James Forbes & Sons, Merchants
   and Wholesale Warehousemen.

   He followed early in life in his father's footsteps, taking an
   active part in Imperial politics. Became a member of the
   Committee of the Conservative Club, and was for seven years
   Vice-President of the Conservative Association, retiring in 1897.
   For two consecutive years, 1887-1889, President of the Aberdeen

25

Chamber of Commerce (incorporated); President, 1895-6, 1896-7, of the Philosophical Society; and Vice-President, 1897-98, of the University Club; Member of Council of the New Spalding Club since 1898. Author of several political and economic pamphlets, including "Political Principles *versus* Practice," published in 1882; "Is Free Trade sound policy for Great Britain?" 1882, delivered to the Aberdeen Philosophical Society—a work which ran through four editions within twelve months, largely interesting political economists throughout Scotland and England, and eliciting many rejoinders from the Cobden Club and Free Traders all over the Kingdom; "Radicals: what they are, and what they want," 1884; "Conservatism," 1885; "How its Fiscal Policy may affect the prosperity of a Nation," 1885; read before the Economic Science Section of the British Association meeting in Aberdeen; "Free Imports and Agricultural Ruin, or Protection and Prosperity," 1888, and other brochures on political economy and contemporary politics.

4. JOHN, born in Kingsland House, Aberdeen, 4th February, 1838, was educated at the Town's Public Schools, the Grammar School, Marischal College and University. After leaving the University he became an articled apprentice to Yeats & Flockhart, advocates in Aberdeen, 1855-60. Brown prizeman for Conveyancing, 1858; for Scotch Law, 1858-9; and for Medical Logic, 1859-60. Entered at Lincolns Inn, 1860; Certificate of Honour, 1st class, 1862; Studentship of Four Inns of Court, June, 1862; called to English Bar in 1862, went the Northern and afterwards the North-Eastern Circuits. Was appointed Council to the Treasury in Mint prosecutions at the West Riding of Yorkshire Sessions and Assizes, by Sir Roundel Palmer, then Attorney-General, in 1865, and held that office till 1878. Was Commissioner for the trial of municipal election petitions from 1885 till 1893. Was a Royal Commissioner of Assize in 1896 (Welsh Circuit); and again in November, 1902, the Lord Chancellor appointed him Commissioner of Assize on the Oxford Circuit, on which he was associated at Birmingham with the Lord Chief Justice of England. He was, in succession to Lord

ALEXANDER FORBES OF MORKEU
1814—1893

JOHN FORBES, K.C.
1838—1904

Macnaghten, appointed Keeper of the Black Books, thereby becoming an official of Lincolns Inn, and in succession to the Treasurership of the Inn, an office greatly coveted, being the highest at the disposal of the Benchers and only held for one year. For six years a member of the Bar Committee; Solicitor-General of the County Palatine of Durham, 1886-87 ; Attorney-General, 1887 to 1900. Created a Q.C., 1881 ; Bencher of Lincolns Inn, 1884 ; Recorder of Hull since December, 1887. Had for many years a large practice as a Junior, and was afterwards leader of his circuit till he retired from practice, 4th February, 1898. He published, in 1875, along with William Wyllys Mackeson, Q.C., " The Judicature Acts and Rules, with forms of pleadings, &c.," which became a standard work.

He was frequently solicited to enter Parliament by several constituencies in England, and for Kincardineshire and South Aberdeen, but he had no taste for a political life. He was invited in 1885 to contest the Kirkcaldy Burghs in the interests of the Established Church of Scotland in opposition to Sir George Campbell, the sitting member, and went the length of delivering six addresses in the principal Burghs, but he found so much apathy among those from whom he expected support, that he did not prosecute his canvas. He was strongly of opinion that lawyers were about the worst representatives any constituency could have, as they generally entered Parliament to promote their own advancement, which in order to secure, they found it necessary to support their party whether consistent with their constituents' interests or otherwise. He loved his native country, and generally spent several months in the autumn in Scotland in shooting and fishing, both of which sports he greatly enjoyed.

He married, in 1866, Maria Elizabeth, younger daughter of Henry Thomas, F.R.C.S., of Sheffield, and had one daughter,

(1). LAURA, married, 30th April, 1902, to Langton Prendergast Walsh, C.I.E., of Laragh, King's Court, Co. Cavan, Ireland, and Ealing, Middlesex,[1] issue—one daughter,

1 Cf. Who's Who, 1904.

27

i. ELEANOR EUPHEMIA ELIZABETH WALSH, born
1903, in India.

John Forbes died 18th March, 1904, and was interred in St.
Nicholas Churchyard.

5. AGNES, the elder daughter, was educated at Miss Lambert's school
and the West End Academy, at that time under Dr. Ferguson, a
most popular teacher, acquiring Latin, Greek, French, and afterwards the German language under Miss McDonald, who later
became the wife of Robert Fletcher, a well-known accountant
and stockbroker in Aberdeen and London. Agnes married, on
25th September, 1855, Archibald Simpson, M.D., and accom-
panied him to Syria, where he held the appointment of surgeon
to the English Hospital, Jerusalem. On Dr. Simpson's return
from the East, he practised as a physician in London for fifteen
years, and died there at the early age of 42 in 1872. Dr. Simpson
left eight children, five sons and three daughters, two boys having
died in infancy. After her husband's death Mrs. Simpson and
family removed to Aberdeen, remaining there for nine years,
when they moved to Edinburgh, where her eldest son, Alexander
James, was in Messrs. Lindsay, Haldane & Jamieson's office
learning to be a chartered accountant. Mrs. Simpson and family
remained in Edinburgh till June, 1887, when they all returned to
London and settled in Putney :—

(1) ALEXANDER JAMES SIMPSON, the eldest son, was born in
Canonbury 21st February, 1858. He was educated in
London at a private school, and afterwards attended
the Law classes at the University of Edinburgh. He
was for four years in the Life department of the
Northern Assurance Co., and afterwards a pupil in
Lindsay, Haldane & Jamieson's office, who were the
leading accountants at that time in Edinburgh, where
he remained nine years. He went to London in 1887,
and was for several years Accountant to the In-
dustrial and General Trust Co. He married, in 1896,
Georgina E. M. Carr, only child of the late Dr. George

28

ESLIE GORDON MORGAN FORBES

1833—1902

AGNES FORBES SIMPSON

ARCHIBALD FORBES SIMPSON

HENRY SIMPSON

Carr, R.N., by his wife, Elizabeth Farquhar, daughter of Nathaniel Farquhar, Advocate in Aberdeen. He was for five years a private in the V. B. of the Gordon Highlanders in Aberdeen. He died 15th June, 1903.

(2). ARCHIBALD FORBES SIMPSON, the second son, was born in Canonbury, London, 9th March, 1859; educated at a private school, and afterwards at the Grammar School and University of Aberdeen. He was for seven years an apprentice and clerk in the Union Bank of Scotland in Aberdeen. He returned to London in 1881, and has been for twenty-three years in the Capital and Counties Bank there, where he is now Chief Inspector. He has been a volunteer for twenty-two years, first in the Gordon Highlanders in Aberdeen, then in the London Scottish, and afterwards Captain in the 3rd V.B. West Kent Regiment. He has the long service medal. In 1904 he was elected a member of the Junior Carlton Club.

(3). HENRY SIMPSON, the third son, was born in Canonbury, London, 22nd October, 1868; educated at the Royal High School, Edinburgh. He was for four years in the Royal Bank of Scotland, in Edinburgh, and afterwards entered the Capital and Counties Bank in London, where he is now manager of the Westminster branch. He was for some years a volunteer in the London Scottish. He married, in 1898, Amian Mary, youngest daughter of Sir Frederick Lacy Robinson, K.C.B., Deputy Chairman of the Board of Inland Revenue, Somerset House, and has issue—

　　i. ARCHIBALD LACY FORBES SIMPSON, born 4th February, 1900.
　　ii. JULIA MARY SIMPSON, born 30th May, 1898.
　　iii. STELLA AMIAN SIMPSON, born 30th May, 1904.

(4). CHARLES JOSEPH FARRINGTON SIMPSON, born in Canonbury, London, 4th March, 1870; educated at the Royal High School, Edinburgh, has been for some years in the London branch of the Life Association of Scotland. He was for five years a member of the London Scottish Volunteers.

(5) JOHN ARCHIBALD FORBES SIMPSON, the youngest son, was born in Canonbury, 11th January, 1873; educated at the Royal High School, Edinburgh, and the City of London School. He was for ten years a member of the London Scottish Volunteers. He is a member of the London Stock Exchange. He married, in 1900, Ethel Newton Scott, by whom he has one daughter,

  i. JEAN NEWTON SIMPSON, born 2nd April, 1902.

(6) ALICE GORDON MORGAN SIMPSON, the eldest daughter, was born in Canonbury; educated in London and Aberdeen.

(7) AGNES MARY SIMPSON, the second daughter, was born in Canonbury; educated at the Ladies' College, Edinburgh. She married, in 1886, Arthur Charles Frederick Dundas, eldest son of General Charles Stirling Dundas, R.A., of Dundas Castle, Linlithgowshire, and was left a widow in the same year.

(8) ANNIE MARJORY SIMPSON, the youngest daughter, born in Canonbury; educated at the Ladies' College, Edinburgh, and the South West London College, Putney.

6. ELSIE GORDON MORGAN, born 21st April, 1833; educated at Miss Lambert's School and the West-End Academy; died 14th November, 1902. She took a warm interest in most local and many national philanthropic institutions, to which she contributed during her life, and by her will left several handsome bequests. Aware that five generations of our family were buried in the same enclosure in St. Nicholas Churchyard, over whom no stone had been erected, she left by bequest £150 to place a memorial stone over the vaults in which they are interred. It bears the following inscription:—

1 ALBYN TERRACE

KINGSLAND HOUSE

Forbes of Forbesfield

SACRED TO THE MEMORY OF
ALEXANDER FORBES IN NEW BALGONEN, KEIG,
SECOND SON OF WILLIAM FORBES SIXTH OF NEWE
BORN 22ND DECEMBER 1687 ; DIED 4TH AUGUST 1740
AND
MARGARET GELLAN HIS WIFE, DIED 30TH NOVEMBER 1752.

JOHN FORBES OF FORBESFIELD, BURGESS IN ABERDEEN
SON OF ABOVE DIED 10TH JANUARY 1785 AND
ANNE FERGUSON HIS WIFE BORN 1738 DIED 28TH MARCH 1792.
ALSO OF THEIR SONS
JOHN, LIEUTENANT 53RD FOOT—BORN 20TH MAY 1774
DIED ABROAD,
ROBERT, LIEUTENANT, H.E.I.C. BORN 27TH APRIL 1780, DIED 27TH OCTOBER 1804.

JAMES FORBES OF FORBESFIELD, MERCHANT IN ABERDEEN,
SON OF ABOVE ; BORN 4TH JULY 1777 DIED 24TH OF MAY 1834
AND
ELIZABETH FRASER HIS WIFE, DIED 27TH DECEMBER 1818.
ALSO THEIR SON JOHN BORN 4TH JULY 1807 DIED 22ND AUGUST 1834

[*On the south side panel*]—
JAMES FORBES MERCHANT IN ABERDEEN,
FOR MANY YEARS A MAGISTRATE OF THE CITY AND JUSTICE OF PEACE
FOR THE COUNTY ; ELDEST SON OF JAMES FORBES AND ELIZABETH FRASER
BORN 15TH JULY 1800, DIED 29TH DECEMBER 1870 ; AND
ELSPET GORDON MORGAN HIS WIFE, BORN 1805 DIED 3RD MAY 1856

[*On the north side panel*]—
ALSO TO THE CHILDREN OF
JAMES FORBES AND ELSPET GORDON MORGAN—
ELSIE MORGAN BORN 21ST APRIL 1833, DIED 14TH NOVEMBER 1902
—THIS MONUMENT WAS ERECTED BY HER BEQUEST—

JOHN FORBES K.C. RECORDER OF HULL,
BORN 4TH FEBRUARY 1838 DIED 18TH MARCH 1904

31

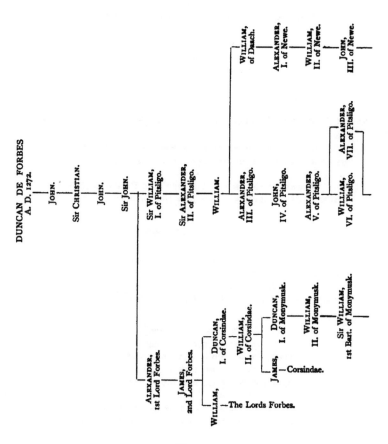

DUNCAN DE FORBES
A. D. 1272.

JOHN.

Sir CHRISTIAN.

JOHN.

Sir JOHN.

Sir WILLIAM, I. of Pitsligo.

Sir ALEXANDER, II. of Pitsligo.

WILLIAM.

WILLIAM, of Dauch.

ALEXANDER, I. of Newe.

WILLIAM, II. of Newe.

JOHN, III. of Newe.

ALEXANDER, III. of Pitsligo.

JOHN, IV. of Pitsligo.

ALEXANDER, V. of Pitsligo.

WILLIAM, VI. of Pitsligo.

ALEXANDER, VII. of Pitsligo.

ALEXANDER, 1st Lord Forbes.

JAMES, 2nd Lord Forbes.

DUNCAN, I. of Corsindae.

WILLIAM, II. of Corsindae.

DUNCAN, I. of Monymusk.

WILLIAM, II. of Monymusk.

Sir WILLIAM, 1st Bart. of Monymusk.

JAMES, —Corsindae.

WILLIAM, —The Lords Forbes.

32

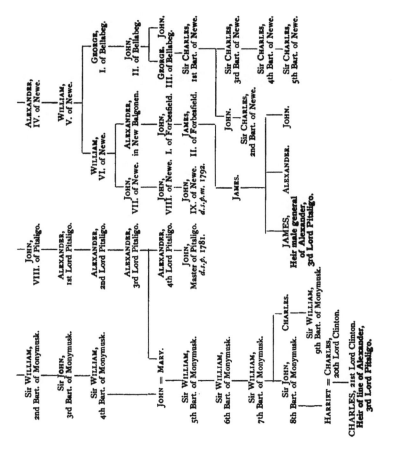

Forbes Appendices

A. Inscription on Tombstone of Alexander Forbes, New Balgonen, in Churchyard of Forbes.

" Here lyes Alexander Forbes Farmer and Square Wright in New-Balgonen who departed this life August the 4 day in the year of God 1740 aged 53 and his children Alexander—Anne—as also Alexander Gellan and Margaret Morgan his Father and Mother in Law."

B. Memorandum by Francis Forbes, Writer.

Francis Forbes, Writer, in a memorandum, instructs Betty Fraser, his spouse—in case she survive him—John Forbes his brother and George Donaldson and Patrick Booth, merchants in Aberdeen, whom he has nominated and appointed to be Tutors and Curators to Margaret and Betty Forbes, his children.

I. As to the said Margaret Forbes, there is a bond of Provision in her favour dated 9th, and Registrate in the Sheriff Court Books of Aberdeen 10th March, 1761, whereby she is provided to 2000 merks in certain events.

V. That all moneys due by bill be called in how soon due and the bills already due not to be renewed. The debt due by the heirs of James Christy by Decrees of Constitution must be insisted for strenuously, and if not paid, the heritage must be adjudged for payment. The debt due by William and Thomas Glennie must also be insisted for in a process against William, and the Trustees of Thomas, viz. :—James Ramsay, advocate, and Francis Leys and George Wilson, merchants—As also the debt due by Robert Turner, Sheriff Substitute, must be immediately insisted for and payment forced without any ceremony, or sufficient security obtained—the sum is pretty large, and it will need force to obtain satisfaction. If any action is necessary for obtaining payment of this debt, I would advise by all means to bring it before the Court of Session, because, he being Sheriff, it cannot come before that Court, and the Commissary Court cannot judge for so large a sum, and the Baillie Court is only a place for boys to play in.

XIV. By the settlement of these heritages being to the longest liver of me and my said spouse in life rent, and to heirs and assignees of the longest liver whatsomever in fee. If my said spouse do survive me, and the said Betty Forbes our daughter—then at her death the whole would by force of the law go to her other nearest relations. In that case she has already solemnly promised, immediately on the death of me and the said Betty Forbes, to grant a settlement of the whole heritable and moveable subjects which shall be pertaining to her at the time of her death, in favour of the said Margaret Forbes, her heirs or Assignees whatsomever. Along with this promise, I hereby leave it on her, as a part of my dying charge, requiring not to go back on her promise, and it is the least in justice she can do in return for my leaving her my all, at own disposal, after she is honestly served herself, to return what remains to my other child, and failing her to my other relations . . . It may be necessary, however, that this be kept in mind, and immediately on her daughter's death to put her in mind of her promise, and then get her to grant a general conveyance of all heritable and moveable subjects that may be pertaining to or resting to her at the time of her death, in favour of the said Margaret Forbes her heirs and assignees whatsomever.

C. Ante-nuptial Bond of Provision, John Forbes to Ann Ferguson, 1763.

"KNOW ALL MEN by these presents Me, John Forbes, Aberdeen, Whereas after mature deliberation and consideration had between me and Ann Ferguson, Lawful Daughter of the Deceased Alexander Ferguson, Merchant in Aberdeen. We have resolved to enter into the State of Matrimony ; and to Solemnise the Holy Bond thereof betwixt us with all convenient speed ; and that it is but just and reasonable, that the said Ann Ferguson should be provided for, after my decease in case she shall happen to survive me. Therefore witt ye me to be bound and obliged, Lykeas I the said John Forbes by the tenor hereof, for the love, favour and affection which I have and bear to the said Ann Ferguson my apparent Spouse in contemplation of the said Marriage, and for her better and more comfortable subsistence after my decease in case she survive me (but always with and under, the Declarations, Restrictions, Burthens, and Provisions aftermentioned), Bind and Oblige me my Heirs, Executors, and Successors whatsomever to pay and deliver to the said Ann Ferguson (in case we shall complete the foresaid Bond of Matrimony betwixt us) All and Haill the sum of Ten pounds Sterling money, Yearly and each year during all the days of her natural lifetime after my Decease in case she survive me, and that at two terms in the year, Whitsunday or Martinmas by equal portions beginning the first terms payment thereof at the first term of Whitsunday or Martinmas next, and immediately following my decease, and so forth, Yearly and Termly thereafter during all the days of her Lifetime, with the sum of One Pound Sterling of Liquidate Expenses for each Term's failzie and annual rent of the said Half Yearly Payments from and after the Term of Payment thereof during the not Payment. And such like I the said John Forbes Bind and Oblige me and my foresaids (but always with and under the Restrictions, Declarations, Burthens, and Provisions after-mentioned as said is) To pay and deliver to the said Ann Ferguson (over and above the before mentioned sum of Ten Pounds Sterling of Annuity) The due and ordinary annual rent of whatever portion may fall to her either before or upon the Decease of Margt. Scott her mother, and that at the terms, by the Proportions, under penalty and bearing Annual Rent in manner particularly before mentioned. And for the said Ann Ferguson her further security and better payment of the Life Rent Annuity before mentioned, I Bind and oblige me and my foresaid to settle and secure, upon Land, Bond, or other good Security the sum of Two hundred pounds Sterling money of my own proper means and Effects, over and above the aforesaid Portion falling to the said Ann Ferguson as said is, whatever the sum may be ; And that at the first term of Whitsunday or Martinmas next and immediately following my decease, and take the Rights thereof under Declaration that the same shall not be affectable by any debts or deeds of mine or my foresaids in prejudice of the said Ann Ferguson Anent the payment making to her of the aforesaid Annuity to whatever extent the same may amount. And it is hereby declared that if by misfortunes in Trade or otherwise my stock shall be so reduced at the time of my Death as not to yield the annual sum of Ten pounds Sterling, It shall be Leisom and Lawful for the said Ann Ferguson to uplift such a part of the Principal sum to be settled in manner foresaid, As will make up that sum Yearly, so as her Annuity in any case may not be under Ten pounds Sterling. And in like manner it is hereby Specially Provided and declared that in case there shall happen to be children of the marriage intended to be Solemnised betwixt us on Life at the time of my Death, I the said Ann Ferguson shall be Bound and Obliged as by her acceptation hereof, she Binds and obliges herself to Aliment, Maintain, and Educate the said Children whether one or more till they be able to earn Bread for themselves; and in that case she shall be and is hereby entitled to the Annual Rent of the Whole Stock belonging to me at the time of my Decease and impowers to Intromit with and uplift the same for the purpose aforesaid. And Such Like it is hereby declared that in Case the annual rent of the said whole stock belonging to me shall not be sufficient to support

37

the said Ann Ferguson and the said Child or Children it shall be Liesome and Lawful to her, but only at the sight, by the direction and with the consent of Two of the Nearest of Kin to the said Child or Children on the father and mother sides, to take such a part or portion Yearly from the stock as shall be judged reasonable for that end. And such like it is hereby expressly provided and declared, that in Case the said Ann Ferguson shall enter into a Second marriage while any of the said Children are on Life, the Annuity provided to her in manner foresaid, shall be, and is hereby restricted to Five pounds Sterling yearly from and after the first term of Whitsunday and Martinmas next and immediately following her marrying again, as said is payable at the Terms by the proportions and bearing arent in matter foresaid. And she shall be and is hereby freed and disburdened of the Alimenting and Educating the said Child or Children from and after the said Term at which the Restriction commences ; Or otherwise she shall continue to Aliment and Educate the said Child or Children and be allowed therefore in the Precise terms above mentioned as if she were still un-married in the option of the said nearest of Kin on both sides. Under and upon the which conditions and provisions and with the Restrictions and declarations above written these presents are granted by me and so accepted by the said Ann Ferguson Allenarly and no otherwise, and it is hereby likewise declared that altho' these Presents shall be found in my Custody, or in the custody of any other person, undelivered to the said Ann Ferguson at the time of my Death yet the same shall be deemed a valid and delivered Writ to all intents and purposes with the not delivery whereof I have dispensed and hereby dispense for ever, and for the more Security I consent to the Registration hereof in the Books of Council and Session or others Competent therein to remain for preservation and if needful to have the strength of a decreet Interponed thereto, that all Execution necessary may pass thereon in form as Effiers and thereto I constitute
my Procurators

In Witness whereof I have subscribed these presents (Wrote on this and the Two preceding Pages of this sheet of stamped paper by Francis Forbes writer in Aberdeen) at Aberdeen this ninteenth day of March One Thousand Seven hundred and Sixty Three years before Witnesses Joseph Forbes my Brother and the said Francis Forbes.

So signed—John Forbes, Ana Ferguson.

Joseph Forbes Witness ; Francis Forbes Witness."

D.   Post Nuptial Contract of Marriage betwixt John Forbes and
Anne Ferguson, 1770.

" At Aberdeen the twentieth day of February One Thousand Seven hundred and Seventy two years : In presence of Alexr. Innes Esq. of Breda Commissary of Aberdeen, Compeared Alexr. Lumsden, Advocate, in Aberdeen as Procr. for the after named and designed John Forbes, and Arthur Dingwall Fordyce advocate in Aberdeen as Procr. for the also after named and Designed Anne Ferguson and Alexr. Ferguson and gave in the Post Nuptial Contract of marriage under written desiring the same might be Insert and Registrate in the Commissary Court books of Aberdeen in terms of the Clause of Registration therein contained which desire the Commissary foresaid found reasonable and ordained the same to be done accordingly; of which contract the principal being wrote upon Stamped paper the Tenor follows viz. :

It is matrimonially Contracted, finally ended and agreed upon betwixt John Forbes Aberdeen on the one part and Anne Ferguson now his Spouse, with advice and Consent of Alexr. Ferguson writer in Edinburgh her brother, and the said Alexr. Ferguson for himself, on the other part. Whereas the said John Forbes and Anne Ferguson have been several years married without any contract being executed betwixt them, and the said Alexr. Ferguson having agreed purely from principles of Regard and Affection towards the said Anne Ferguson, his sister, and the Children already Procreate of the marriage between her and the said John Forbes to give to her the sum of Two Thousands Merks Scots in name of Tocher upon the following conditions and provisions communed and agreed upon between him for behoof of his said sister and the said John Forbes, and that a contract should be entered into between them according thereto. Therefore the said John Forbes sensible of the generosity of the said Alexr. Ferguson, and in Implement of his part of the foresaid communing and agreement, and in contemplation of the said marriage and of the Two Thousand merks of Tocher contracted with the said Anne Ferguson, Binds and Obliges himself his heirs, Executors and Successors against the different terms after mentioned to have in readiness of his own proper means and effects the respective Sums of money following viz. : The sum of Four Thousand Merks Scots Money against the term of Martinmas in this present year One Thousand seven hundred and seventy which together with the Two thousand Merks of Tocher before mentioned making together the sum of Six Thousand merks Scots, he binds and obliges himself and his forsaids to ware and stock out at the said Term upon Land, Bond or other sufficient security ; and a further sum of Two Thousand merks Scots money more at the first term of Whitsunday or Martinmas immediately after the death of the said John Forbes in case he shall predecease the said Anne Ferguson making in whole the said Three sums the sum of Eight Thousand merks Scots money and to take the Rights of the Six Thousand Merks conceived to himself and the said Anne Ferguson and the longest liver of them two in cojunct fee and life-rent for Security to her Allinarly of the sum of Twenty pounds Sterling of Annuity hereafter provided to her and to the Children already procreate or that shall be procreate between them in fee and the Rights of the Two Thousand merks more to the said Anne Ferguson only in case she survive the said John Forbes, and how oft the said respective sums of Six Thousand Merks or Eight Thousand merks or any part thereof shall be uplifted; as oft and of new to Re-employ the same and take the rights and securities thereof devised as aforesaid Which Life Rent Annuity of Twenty pounds Sterling the said John Forbes in the event of his predecease Binds and Obliges him, his Heirs and Successors whatever to content and pay to the said Anne Ferguson during her life-time and Widowity free of all deductions or burthens whatsoever at two terms in the year Whitsunday and Martinmas by equal portions beginning the first term Payment thereof at the first term of Whitsunday or Martinmas which shall happen after his decease for the Half year immediately preceding and so forth yearly and termly thereafter during her Lifetime, with a fifth part more of each moiety of Penalty in case of fallzie and the due and ordinary Annual rent of the said moieties from and after the prospective terms of payment until payment of the same. But in case the said Anne Ferguson shall enter into a second marriage during the Lifetime of any of the Children Procreate or to be Procreate of this marriage. Then and in that event her foresaid annuity of Twenty pounds Sterling is hereby restricted to an Annuity of Fifteen pounds Sterling to commence and be payable from the first term of Whitsunday or Martinmas after her entering into such second marriage with advent and a proportional penalty in case of not punctual payment at the respective terms of Martinmas and Whitsunday before mentioned. And the said John Forbes hereby reserves power to himself to divide the said Sum of Eight Thousand merks provided to the Children of this marriage among them in such proportions as he shall think fit by a writing under his hand any time in his life, and failing thereof, he hereby gives power to the said Anne Ferguson in case she survive him, and be un married to make such division of the same amongst them by a writing under her hand at any time in her life, which also failing, then the said sum is to fall equally among the said children share and share alike. But if the said marriage shall dissolve, by the predecease of the said Anne Ferguson

without issue procreate and existing thereof at the time of her death then and in
that case the said John Forbes binds and obliges, him, his Heirs, and Successors
whatever to make payment to the said Alexr. Ferguson, his Heirs, Executors, or
Assigns of the sum of One Thousand merks, Scots, being the one half of the said
portion hereafter conveyed and that at the first term of Whitsunday or Martinmas
which shall happen after the decease of the said Anne Ferguson with a fifth part
more of penalty in case of failzie and the due and ordinary Annualrent of the said
One Thousand merks after the term of payment of the same in the event before
mentioned until payment thereof. And moreover whatever lands, Heritages,
Debts and sums of money, Goods, and Gear, whatsomever, the said John Forbes
shall purchase or acquire during the standing of this Marriage, and be worth at
the time of the Dissolution thereof, over and above the sum of Eight Thousand
merks before mentioned, the surplus or excess shall be esteemed the conquest of
this marriage and the said John Forbes hereby reserves full power to dispose upon
the said conquest as he shall think proper. And likewise the said John Forbes
hereby assigns and makes over to the said Ann Ferguson in case she shall survive
him, and that there be Children, one or more existing at the Dissolution of the
marriage, the just and equal half, and in case of no Children existing as said is or
their Dying in minority and unmarried before their said Mother, the whole of his
household furniture, Bed and Table Linen, Webs cut and uncut, Silverplate,
Books, Pictures, and Tea Equipage, Heirship Moveables included, which
Assignation to the household plenishing whether half, or whole, the said John
Forbes Binds and Obliges him and his foresaids to warrand at all hands and to
free and disburthen the same of all debts and incumbrances which shall or may
any ways interfere with her peaceable possession thereof, which life rent and other
provisions above written the said Anne Ferguson with consent of her said brother
takes and accepts of in full of all Terce of Lands, Third or Half of moveables
Exery. and others whatsoever which she can ask or Crave by and through the
Death of the said John Forbes before her, or which her Executors or nearest in
kin can claim or demand from the said John Forbes in case he shall survive her;
except what further he shall of his own Good Will provide to her. For the which
Causes and on the other part the said Alexr. Ferguson In Implement of his part
of the foresaid Communing and agreement makes, Constitutes and Ordains the
said John Forbes and his Heirs the said Alexr. Ferguson's Cissioners and
Assignees in and to the Principal Sum of Eighty Three pounds Three shillings
and two pence Sterling and like wis in and to the principal sum of Twenty Seven
pounds, nineteen shillings and one penny Sterling making together the sum
of One Hundred and Eleven pounds Two shillings and Three pence Sterling or

Two Thousand merks Scots of Tocher before mentioned, contained in two seperate Bonds granted to the said Alexr. Ferguson by James Huie, merchant, in Nether Mills of Strath Isla, both date the ninth day of November One Thousand Seven hundred and Sixty two years and Registrate in the Commissary Court Books of Aberdeen the Twenty first day of December said year, and in, and to the Respective penalties contained in the said bonds and annualrent of the principal sums hereby assigned from and after the term of Martinmas last One Thousand Seven hundred and Sixty nine years and in all time thereafter, and in and to the Letters of Inhibition raised by the said Alexr. Ferguson against the said James Huie upon the said Two Bonds with the Execution thereof duly registrate in the General Register at Edinburgh the Thirteenth day of April One Thousand Seven hundred and Sixty four years with all that has followed or is competent to follow thereon Surrogating and Substituting the said John Forbes and his foresaids in the said Alexr. Ferguson's full right and place of the premises forever. Which Assignation the said Alexr. Ferguson Binds and obliges him to warrand from his own proper facts and deeds Allenarly. And He hath instantly delivered to the said John Forbes an extract of each of the foresaids Bonds and principal Letters of Inhibition and Executions on the Back to be kept and used by him and his foresaids as their own Property in time to come which Provision the said Ann Ferguson with consent of the said John Forbes her husband accepts of in full of all Bairns part of Gear, Portion, Natural Legittim and of all she can claim from the same Alexr. Ferguson any manner of way. And Lastly it is agreed that all Execution Competent for implement of the Provisions herein contained in favour of the said Anne Ferguson, and the issue of this marriage shall pass at the instance of the said Alexr. Ferguson and his Heirs and the said parties Consent to the Registration hereof in the Books, of Council and Session or others Competent for preservation, or if necessary that Letters of Horning and all other Execution needful may be directed thereupon in form as effiers and for that effect they constitute

their Prors. and in witness whereof they have subscribed these presents Written by Whitehall Alexr. Duncan apprentice to Arthur Dingwall Fordyce of Culsh advocate in Aberdeen upon this and the six preceeding pages of Stamped paper as Follows viz. : by the said John Forbes and Ann Ferguson at Aberdeen the Third day of November One Thousand Seven hundred and Seventy years before Witnesses the said Arthur Dingwall Fordyce, and Whitehall Alexr. Duncan, and by the said Alexr. Ferguson at Edinburgh the fifteenth day of November in the year One Thousand Seven hundred and Seventy before witnesses Captain James Ferguson of his Majesty's navy and Mr. Alexr. Dallas Silk

Dyer in Edinburgh the day of the month, Witnesses names, and designations being filled up by the said Alexr. Ferguson.

(Signed) John Forbes, Anna Ferguson, Alexr. Ferguson.

Ar. Dingwall Fordyce Witness, W. Alexr. Duncan Witness, Alexr. Dallas Witness, James Ferguson Witness."

E. Nomination of Tutors by John Forbes, 1782.

"At Aberdeen the twelfth day of October One Thousand Seven hundred and Eighty five years : In presence of Alexander Elphinstone Esquire advocate Sheriff Depute of Aberdeenshire, Compeared the after designed David Morrice and gave in the nomination of Tutors and Curators under-written, Desiring that the same might be Insert and Registered in his Ldship. Court Books in terms of the Clause of Registration therein contained which desire the said Sheriff found Reasonable and ordained the said nomination of Tutors and Curators to be Registered accordingly, and of which the principal being written on Stamped paper the tenor follows viz. :—

"I John Forbes Aberdeen having entire confidence in the Fidelity, Care, and Diligence of Alexander Ferguson writer in Edinburgh, Patrick Booth Merchant in Aberdeen, Thomas Taylor wright in Aberdeen, and David Morrice Junr. Advocate in Aberdeen, for executing the trust after-mentioned, Do hereby nominate and appoint them the said Alexander Ferguson, Patrick Booth, Thomas Taylor and David Morrice Junr., and each of them to be Tutors and Curators To Mary, John, James, and Robert Forbes's my Children during all the days of their Pupilarity and minority after my Decease with full power to them. Three of them always being a Quorum to take the management of the persons, means and Effects of my said Children during the period aforesaid. And to do everything concerning the same which the Laws of Scotland authorises Tutors and Curators nominate to do. But declaring hereby that they nor neither of them their Heirs, nor Executors are to be charged with any omission concerning the said Tutory or Curatory, whereof they and each of them as hereby Exonered and Discharged forever. And that it shall be no-ways necessary for them to make up Tutorial or Curatoriall Inventorys of my said Children's means and Effects, but that Inventorys thereof signed by them or their Quorum shall be sufficient, notwithstanding any Law to the contrary and in regard I am desirous that my said Children should during the Pupilarities and minorities be always under the care and management of Four Honest men, therefore how soon any of the Four persons above-mentioned shall be called off by Death I hereby fully Authorise and Impower the Three Surviving to Elect and make Choice of such a person to supply his place as to them shall seem proper and that such Election and Choice shall be made within one month after the Death of the defunct and during the course of the said Period such Election shall be made by the survivors for the time being, on the Death of any of the said Tutors and Curators, Declaring hereby that a minute wrote on the Back hereof or any Sederunt or minute Book kept by the said Tutors or Curators and signed before Witnesses by the electors in token of their choice and by the person Elected, in token of his acceptance shall invest the person Elected, and accepting with all powers hereby granted to the said Alexr. Ferguson, Patrick Booth, Thomas Taylor and David Morrice Junr. to all intents and purposes and it being necessary for several reasons that my said Children remain under the Care of Anne Ferguson my spouse and in family with her during her Life-time if she survive me, I hereby earnestly recommend and request the said Alexander Ferguson, Patrick Booth, Thomas Taylor and David Morrice Junr., and failing any of them those to be chosen in their place in manner foresaid. To advise, Assist, and Direct the said Anne Ferguson in the management of the said Children particularly as to their education and morals, and also of Herself and Her Affairs in General hereby tenderly advising and requesting her to accept off and conduct herself by such advise and assistance, and I recommend to the said Tutors and Curators to sell and Dispose of my Feu at Rubislaw even during the pupilarity and minority of the said Children if the proper opportunity Offers. And Consent to the Registration hereof in the Books of Council and Session or any other Competent Register for preservation and constitute

my Procrs. and in witness whereof I have subscribed these presents Written on this and the two preceeding pages of this sheet of stamped paper by the said David Morrice at Aberdeen the twenty first day of December, One Thousand seven hundred and Eighty two before these Witnesses Samuel Johnstone merchant in Aberdeen and David McAllan shoemaker there.

(Signed) John Forbes.

Samuel Johnstone Witness, David McAllan Witness."

F. Inventory and Appretiation of John Forbes deceased's Household Furniture and other effects taken and made by John Smith, Auctioneer, January 1785.

	DINING ROOM.	£	S	D
Mahogany Desk and Cabinet		6	0	0
A Mahogany Standard		0	18	0

44

Appendices

	£	S	D
A Chest Drawers	1	10	0
A Tea Tray	0	5	0
A Clock	6	0	0
1 Grate, Fender & Fire Irons	0	16	0
6 Chairs Plain and 2 Corner	2	0	0
1 Dining Table	1	10	0
1 Looking Glass	1	10	0
1 Floor Cloth	0	15	0
1 Bellows	0	0	6
Do.	0	3	0
1 Watch			

BOOKS IN DRAWERS.

	£	S	D
1 Bible Quarto	0	5	0
Baxters Ch. Directory	0	2	0
Fountain of Life	0	0	6
Ambrose Works	0	3	0
Cartwright on New Testament	0	0	8
Image of the Beast	0	0	6
Expla. of Philippians	0	0	2
Do. of Colossians	0	0	2
Dr. Buchans Works	0	4	0
Manton on Isaia	0	1	0
Gibson on Temptation	0	1	0
Dickson on Sermons	0	0	6
Light of Nature by Colverwells	0	0	2
Haliburtons Concern	0	0	6
Arithmetic by Halway	0	0	6

BOOKS.

	£	S	D
Boston on the Covenant of Grace . . .	0	0	6
Ferguson on the Galatians and Ephesians . .	0	0	6
Willisens Chatechism	0	0	2
Tiltens Sermon	0	0	6
Bostons Four fold State	0	0	8
Sherlock on Death	0	0	6
Spectator 8 vols.	0	5	0
Flavilla on Redemption	0	1	0
Baxter agt. Johnston	0	0	2

	£	S	D
Vindication of Dissenters	0	0	6
Volume of Sermons	0	0	4
A Sermon by Wilson	0	0	6
Harvies Sermons	0	1	0
Marishalls on Sanctification	0	0	6
Harvies Works 2 vols.	0	1	6
Theron & Aspasio by Hewey 2 vols. . . .	0	1	6
Essay	0	0	3
Arnet on Christianity	0	0	8
Rutherfords Letters vols. 2 and 3	0	1	0
Confession of Faith	0	1	0

BEDROOM.

	£	S	D
Six Elm Chairs	0	18	0
1 Mirror Glass	0	16	0
1 Chest Drawers	1	1	0
1 Tea Chest and 3 Cannisters	0	4	0
1 Grate, Fender & Irons	0	15	0
1 Cupboard	0	3	0
A Bed Stead & Casters	2	0	0
Two and ½ pair Blankets	1	0	0
Two Feather Beds, 2 Bolsters & 4 Pillows . .	4	4	0
1 Quilled Cover	0	16	0
1 Pair Sheets	0	6	0
1 China Punch and State Bowl	0	5	0
2 Stone tea Pots	0	1	0
2 Small China Bowls	0	7	0
1 large Do. Do.	0	8	0
10 Cups and Saucers, 1 Tea Pot, 1 Milk Pot, and Sugar Box and State Bowls	0	7	0
3 Stone Cups and Saucers and Pewtor Tankard . .	0	1	4
12 Tea and Sugar Spoons	1	1	0
6 Silver Table Spoons and Dividing Spoon . .	6	10	0
6 Breakfast Knives, Silver Hafted Kitchen . .	0	2	6

KITCHEN.

	£	S	D
1 Grate, Tongs Shovel and Poker . . .	0	8	0
2 Choffurs	0	5	0

	£	S	D
2 Tea Kettles and Coffee Pot	0	10	0
4 Candlesticks	0	6	0
2 Pewtor Basins and Tankard	0	1	6
3 Brass Pans	0	5	0
1 Wort Pan, 2 Metal pots and Kettle Pot · . .	0	5	0
1 Large Copper Pot and Cover and Goblet . . .	0	10	0
1 Brander and 1 Lamp	0	1	0
1 Sown Bowie, 1 Girdle, 1 Frying Pan and Hatchet .	0	4	0
1 Bellows, 1 Bread Toaster, 1 Salt Backet, Spit and Raxes .	0	6	0
1 Buckett and 2 Small tubs	0	2	0
2 Flesh Baskets, Baking Case and Board . .	0	4	0
1 Pewter Salvor, 1 Drainer, Bread, Spurtle and Flesh forks .	0	2	0
1 Brander and Kettle Stand . . .	0	3	0
1 Sugar Grater, 2 Pudding Pans and 1 Flaggon . .	0	1	6
2 Pewter Plates and Six Pewter Trunchers . .	0	6	0
4 Dozn. Yellow Stone Trunchers	0	6	0
1 Knife Box and 12 Knives and forks . . .	0	4	6
1 Gro. Chopine Bottles	0	18	0
5 Stools and Small Screen	0	1	8
2 Pairs Blankets and Cover in Bed . . .	0	15	0
1 Chaff Bed and Bolster	0	3	0
1 Sheet	0	1	6
1 Cran 6d. 1 Coal backet 6d. . . .	0	1	0

COOM CEILED ROOM.

	£	S	D
1 Wainscote Table	0	3	0
Tent Bed and Curtains	2	0	0
2 Feather Beds, 1 Bolster and 2 Pillows . . .	3	0	0
1 Press	0	5	0
1 Desk and Bookcase Old	1	1	0
1 Press	0	4	0
1 Box Bed	0	4	0
1 Old Stooped Bed	0	2	6
2 Wheels, 1 Reel, and 1 Muckle Wheel . . .	0	5	6
2 Chaff Beds and 2 Bolsters	0	4	0
2 Harden Sheets	0	2	0
Pair Blankets and 2 Covers	1	12	0

	£	S	D
6 Table Cloths	1	4	0
3 dozn. Tervits and 2 Table Cloths	1	16	0
2 Small Table Cloths and 18 Table Napkins	0	14	0
5 Pair Linnen Sheets	2	0	0
1 dozn. White Pillow Cases	1	0	0
2 Pairs Harden Sheets	0	6	0
12 Single Sheets	1	10	0
2 Butter Kitts	0	2	0
2 Beef Casks	0	3	0

NURSERIE.

	£	S	D
1 Easy Chair	1	0	0
1 Bed Stead and Curtains	0	4	0
1 Feather Bed, 1 Bolster, and 2 Pillows	2	0	0
1 Chaff Bed	0	2	0
2 Pair and One Single Blanket	1	4	0
1 Sheet and Cover	0	3	0
1 Box Bed	0	3	0
1 Chaff Bed and Feather Bolster	0	5	0
3 Pair Blankets	1	4	0
1 Sheet	0	1	6
2 Stools 1 Small Chair and 1 Old Chest	0	3	0
1 Box Iron Heaters and Standard	0	3	0
1 Hen Crieve, 4 Washing tubs and 2 Stools	0	5	6

BREW HOUSE.

	£	S	D
7 Ankers	0	4	6
1 Brew Vatt and Stool	0	3	0
1 Half Hogshead and 2 Working Stands	0	6	0
1 large Crock 2/- 5 Meal Casks and Covers 10/-	0	12	0

WEARING APPARELLE.

	£	S	D
3 Wigs and Box	0	6	0
1 Pair Shoe and 1 pair knee Buckles	0	15	0
1 pair Peeble Buttons	0	2	0
1 Suit Black Clothes	1	0	0
1 Suit Lead Colour	0	10	0
1 Do. Parson Grey	0	10	0
3½ dozn. Day Shirts	3	10	0

				£	S	D
1½ dozn. Muslin Cravats .	.	.	.	1	0	0
2 Flannel Shirts 2/- 8 pair Stockings 8/- .	.	.	.	0	10	0
3 Jappaned Salvers . .	.	.	.	0	3	0
2 Wine Decanters and 2 Stone Mugs .	.	.	.	0	2	6
	Total	.	.	£85	12	3

G. John Forbes deceased. List of Bills, January, 1785.

Also there was found in the Defuncts Repositories

In Cash	£40 0 0
Item Bill Robt. Balmano, 6th Jan., 1785, payable 20 Dec. 1785	£52 10 0
Item promisary Robt. Balmano 6th Jany. 1785 payable on demand	£4 0 0
Bill Al. and Jo. Forbes of Invererman Dated 24th Decm. 1783 payable 21 Dec. 1784 . . .	£52 10 0
Bill Dav. Morice Junr. Dated 20 Decm. 1784 payable 20 Dec. 1785	£315 0 0
Bill Al. Duffes and Alexr. Martin Dated 20 June 1784 payable 20th June 1785	£105 0 0
Bill Ann and Jean Yeats Dated 21st June 1784 payable 21 June 1785	£63 0 0
Bill Margte. Luckie Dated 13 Augst. 1784 payable Six Months after Date	£7 3 6
Bill Al. Ferguson Dated 6th Feb. 1782 payable at 1782	£51 5 0
Bill Dav. Sheriff Junr. Dated 20th Augt. 1774 payable 6 months after Date . . .	£1 18 0
Bill Mary Ferguson and Margaret Black Dated 12th Jan. 1784 payable 20th June 1784 . . .	£24 0 0
Bill Mary Ferguson and Margt. Black Dated 12 Jan. 1784 payable 20th June 1784 . . .	£30 15 0
Bill Wm. Duff 24 Dec. 1784 payable upon 20 Decm. 1784 .	£5 10 0
Item Amount of Shoes Delivered to Dr. Alex. Clerk on his going to Jamaica with his obligation on the foot to Dispose of the shoes and remitte for the produce Dated 6 Septr. 1783	£44 2 0

Item Letter of Relief Robt. Luckie Relative to Sundries Bills
for which Mr. Forbes is Security amounting to
£94 . 1 . 10 as Letter of Relief and obligation Mary
Black, Jas. Black, Margt. Ferguson and Margt. Black
relatives to a Legacy of £30 received on Mary Black
account Dated 12th Jany. 1784.

Obligation D. Morice Senr. relative to one pound Sterling left in
his hands 24th Decr. 1783.

Bill Angus McLean Dated 16th Feby., 1779 payable on Demand
with protest thereon Balance due . . . £1 10 6

Bill Hugh Ross Dated 20th Jany. 1781 payable 20th June
thereafter Ball. due £1 11 10

Bill John and And. Websters Dated 1st May 1781 payable 3
months after date £4 9 6

Bill Margt. Mitchell 1766 . . . . . £1 10 0

Bill John Melvin in Auchloneed Dated 29th June 1780 payable
20 Dec. 1780 to protest £3 5 7

Bill Geo. Donald, 1773 . . . . . £5 18 7½

Bill Jas. Wildgoose £1 16 4

Bill Robt. Weir Stornay 1772 . . . . £4 7 8

Bill Robt. Shill as 1773 . . . . . £0 13 6

State of Debts by John Gray Edn. the Bill supposed to be at
Edn. £8 4 1

In the Defunct's Pocket Book Cash . . . £3 3 0

Bond James Horne To Alexr. Ferguson Dated 9 Nov. 1762 for
£27 . 19 . 1 payable at 6th March 1802, the rents
payable yearly at the rate of 4½ till the principall fall due.

Inhibition on said Bond assign Alex. Ferguson to John Forbes
of Sundrie Debts owed by Geo. Scott Dated 4th Oct.
1774. In account copy of Submission of Letter from
Al. Ferguson relative to the foresaid Bond.

H. Names of Debtors on the deceased John Forbes' Books: all supposed to be good, January, 1785.

Mrs. Cockburn.	James Chalmers, printer.
Miss Elphinstone.	Mrs. John Byres.
Mrs. Doctor Hay.	Mrs. Baillie Forbes.
Jno. Wallace.	James Aberdein.

Mrs. Culbertson.
Lady Scotstown.
Mr. George Copland.
Mrs. Ogilvie, Auchiries.
Baillie Hadden.
James Frise.
Miss Nancy Harvey.
Mrs. Mark.
Miss Ragg.
Miss Dolly Cummine.
Doctor French.
Doctor Ogilvie.
Mr. Anderson, barber.
Miss Irvine, Cults.
Mrs. Provost Davidson.
Mrs. Knight.
Professor Gordon.
Lady Grandholm, Senr.
Miss Teresa Lumsden.
Mrs. Fyfe, Dudwick.
Lady Frazerfield.
Miss Provost Davidson.
Miss Lumsden, Corachrie.
Mr. Thomas Black.
Convener Smith.
Mr. Langley.
John Blackhall.
Alex. Burgess.
Misses Udnies.
Sir William Seton.
Mrs. Bannerman, Justice Lane.
Misses Pauls
Miss Simpson, Hazelhead.
Lady Avochie.
Mrs. Wm. Thom.
Mr. John Davidson, Tillychetlie.
Lord Forbes.
Mr. Dawney, Banchory.
Misses Turners.

Mr. Garrioch, Old Town.
Peggy Clerk.
Mr. Pirrie, Ellon.
Mr. Davidson, Rayne.
Mr. Forbes, coppersmith.
Mrs. James Black.
Miss William Black.
Mrs. Baillie Burnett.
Mr. William Duguid.
Miss Brownie, Cullen.
Mrs. Dunbar & Mr. Geo. do.
Bell Galloway.
Mr. Lundie, Lonmay.
Mr. John Ross.
Miss Douglas, printer.
Miss Simpson.
Mrs. McCombie.
Miss McVeagh.
Lady Barrack and Misses.
Mrs. Alexander Annand.
Forbes Hay.
William Fiddes.
Miss Betty Innes.
Mrs. Thos. Bannerman.
Mrs. Home.
Mrs. Captain Allan.
Miss Burn.
Mr. Harry Lumsden.
Miss Rachel Seton.
Mr. Samuel Grant.
Capt. Hadden.
Miss Sheperd.
Miss Betty Logie.
Baillie Abercrombie.
Margaret Forbes.
Professor Gerrard.
George Skene.
Baillie Willox.
Mrs. Capt. Campbell,

51

Mrs. Gordon, Ramoir.
Miss Ketty Skene.
Mr. Jas. Boyne.
Annie Lobban.
Lumsden, Cushnie.
Cummine, Pitulie.
Mrs. Winter.
Samuel Johnstone.
John Gordon, Craig.
Mr. Benjamin Kitchen.
Mr. Charles Forbes.
Mr. Copland, Fintray.
Mr. Alex. Lumsden.
Mrs. Farquharson, Antigua.
Mr. McKenzie, Glenmuick.
Captain Rosse.
Mrs. Principal Campbell and Miss F.
Miss Dalziel, Tillery and the Doctor.
Mr. Geo. Forbes.
Sir Edward Bannerman.
Lady Forbes, Fintray.
Mr. Morrice, Kincardine.
Lady Counteswells.
Baillie Garden.
Mr. Cock, Cruden.
Mr. Mosley.
Miss Haggerts.
Provost Cruden.
Dr. Livingston.
Mrs. Dr. Donaldson.
Mr. Geo. Scott.
Patk. Pirie.
Miss R. Skene.
Mr. Patk. Robertson.
Miss Forbes Gordon.
Mr. Peacock.
Mr. Geo. Skene.
Margaret Sherriffs.
Jas. Ross, Schoolmaster.

Mr. Alex. Innes, Garlogie.
Mrs. Gordon, Inchmarlo.
Mrs. Gordon, Senr., Buthlay.
Lieut. Farquharson, Cowly.
Provost Young.
Nelly Reidford.
Miss Thomson.
Miss Abernethy.
Robert Smith.
Mrs. Ballingall.
Misses Glashan.
Mr. Francis Logie.
Miss Moir, Stoneywood.
Miss Peggie Mowat now Mrs. Jamison.
Bell Wishart.
Alex. Simmers, Junr.
Francis Knox.
John Forbes.
Captain Thos. Ogilvie.
Miss Fordyce in Miss Irvines.
Mr. William Young, Counteswells.
Mr. Wm. Fitzgerald.
Mr. Alex. Anderson, merchant.
Miss Glenny.
Relict of Late Minister Udny & Son.
Elisa Edrington.
Alex. Stiven, wright.
Geo. Burnett, Esqr., Kemnay.
Mr. Geo. Forbes, baker.
Lady Reid.
Mrs. Smith, Late of Tillydrone.
Jean Cooper, Putachie.
Helen Cantly.
Saml. Forbes.   Cash Lent.
Miss Farquharson, Terra.
Mr. Charles Taws.
Mrs. Francis Garden.
Hogg of Ramoir, Esqr.
Widow Hardie.

Appendices

Miss Brown, Craigdam.
The Rev. Mr. Wm. Taylor.
William Turner, Balquhain.
Miss Nancy Harvey.
Mrs. Innes, Elgin.
John Grant of Kincardine, Esqr.
Miss Farquhar, New Hall.
John Moir, Gateside.
William Leslie, Garbotie.
Mrs. Lee.
Mr. James Pirie.
Jean Cheyne.
Mr. Young, Printfield.
Pitullie.
Grandholm.
Mr. Grant, Tulloch.
Mr. Forbes, Lochell.
Baillie Robert Cruickshank.
Arthur Dingwall Fordyce.
Mr. David Morrice, Senr.
Provost Duncan.
Miss Buthlay.
Margaret Clerk.
Alex. Cushnie.
Geo. Craig.
Mr William Forbes.
Mrs. Margaret Williamson.
Wm. Smith, merchant, Green.
Alex. Thomson.
Kenneth M'Kenzie.
Jamaica.
Mr Balmanno.
Tillygrig.
Bellabeg.
Foveran.
Strichen.
Kinmundy.
Tillywhilly.
Aberdour.
Kininmonth.

Mrs. Margaret Michie.
William Menzies.
Mr. David Collieson.
Nelly Scott.
Mrs. Wildgoose.
Janet Carmichael.
Mrs. Cavins.
Betty Harper at Tillygrig.
John Lamb with Capt. Cairnie.
Mr. Robert Finnie.
Mr. Alex. Tosh.
Mrs. Orem.
Mr. Milne, Esslemont.
Lady Dudwick.
Mr. Hutcheon, minister.
Mr. Patk. Sandilands.
Mr. Gammack.
Lady Findrick.
Miss Shand.
Mr. Geo. Morrison.
Miss Bell Morrison.
Miss Findlay.
John Gordon, Birkenbush.
Miss Baby Robertson.
Professor Copland.
Craickinara.
Miss Patk. Thomson.
Miss Leith, Freefield.
Miss Professor Gordon.
Miss French.
Memsie.
Lady Ballater.
Rippachie.
Miss Ogston.
Miss Abercrombie.
Mr. James Black, Senr. .
Bruce, wife of T. Johnstone.
Miss Anne Gordon.
Auchiries.
Lady Tannachie.

I. The Tutors of John Forbes' Children in a/c current with David Morice, Jun., their Factor, per his Ledger, 1790-91.

1790.

14 April.	Pd. College Fees for John Forbes . . .	£3	15	8
5 June.	Pd. for John Forbes stamped paper for Indenture .	0	5	0½
13 July.	Pd. for John Forbes dues to the Society of Procurators	1	1	0
17 Augst.	Pd. Miss Leith Milliner apprentice fee for Mary Forbes	3	13	6
6 Decr.	Pd. for John Forbes Porter and Sacrists dues at College	0	5	6
1791.				
15 Jany.	Pd. Cash to David Morice, Advocate, for John Forbes apprentice fee	16	13	4
31 March.	Pd. for College Funds John Forbes . . .	0	3	6
26 May.	Pd. Hugh Murray for Music for Robert while at Mr. Annands Dancing School . . .	0	7	0
26 May.	Pd. Hugh Murray for Month at Dancing School .	0	7	0
8 June.	Pd. for Robert ticket to Mr. Annands ball . .	0	7	0
23 July.	Pd. for Robert for two quarters Dancing to Annand Dancing Master	2	2	0
7 Novr.	Pd. for Robert ticket for Annands Ball . .	0	7	0
21 Novr.	Pd. for Robert quarters fee and fire at Grammar School	0	3	6

J. Items taken from Account Book of Thomas Duncan Advocate in Aberdeen the Factor to the Trustees of the children of the deceased John Forbes Forbesfield, 1792-1801.

1792.

8 April.	Pd. Mr. Duncan Writing Master a quarters education of Robert Forbes	£0	3	6
10 May.	Pd. Mr. Duncan Writing Master for education of James Forbes and Books . . .	0	12	5
16 May.	Pd. for Robert Forbes 1 quarters education at Grammar School	0	2	6
23 June.	Pd. for John Forbes seat rent in church . .	0	2	6
15 Augst.	Pd. Mr. Duncan 1 quarters writing and Arithmetic for James Forbes	0	6	0

54

Date	Description	£	s	d
3 Septr.	Pd. John Forbes cash to purchase a book . .	£0	6	0
22 Decr.	Pd. one years feu duty Forbesfield and stamp .	8	0	2
28 Decr.	Pd. Insurance of Country House . . .	0	3	6
1793.				
30 Jany.	Pd. Expense of making out a well and for pump bricks &c. per a/c	7	8	6
8 April.	Pd. Advertising Country House and Parks . .	0	4	6
13 Feby.	Pd. Robert Forbes for Greek Homer and Fables .	0	7	0
28 Feby.	Pd. Robt. Forbes for locarium dues . . .	0	3	6
1794.				
24 March.	Pd. Professor Stewart College fees for Robert .	2	2	0
12 Septr.	Pd. for Robert a quarters dues at Grammar School .	0	5	0
28 Augst.	Pd. Cameron & McHardy a/c for Miss Forbes .	2	5	0
28 „	Pd. Thomson barber for Robert Forbes . .	0	7	0
18 Septr.	Pd. Advertising Country House . . .	0	9	0
18 Novr.	Pd. Mr. Duncan 1 quarters education for Robert .	0	6	6
21 Novr.	Pd. for Robert Sacrist and porters college dues .	0	5	6
26 Novr.	Pd. do. for paper book and fire . .	0	2	0
1795.				
2 July.	Pd. Taxation and levy money for seamen . .	0	7	1
2 July.	Cash advanced to John Forbes to purchase uniform when he joined Aberdeen Volunteers . .	8	0	0
7 July.	Pd. John Smith auctioneer for roup of parks &c. at Forbesfield	1	15	4
22 Decr.	Pd. James Clark taylor for John Forbes . .	5	8	7
1796.				
14 Decr.	Pd. Mr. Nicholson French Master for Robert Forbes	1	2	0
1799.				
3 Jany.	Pd. Robert Lamb a/c due by Robt. Forbes . .	13	0	8
8 March.	Pd. for linen for shirts to Robt. Forbes . .	2	12	0
8 March.	Pd. Miss Black for making same . . .	0	8	0
10 May.	Pd. Mr. Dun Dancing Master for Robert Forbes .	0	16	0
1801.				
May.	Pd. one years allowance for balancing D. M'Allans books from Jany. 1792 to Jany 1793 . .	4	0	0
May.	By Thomas Duncan Factor fee for 9½ years from Novr. 1791 to May 1801 at £4 4/- yearly .	39	18	0
	By two years Road money	0	12	1½

K. Letters from Robert Forbes, H.E.I.C.S., to James Forbes of Forbesfield, and Samuel Johnston, Aberdeen, 1800.

> 11, Fountain Court Strand
> London,
> 19 April, 1800.

My dear Brother

Your Packet under cover to Mr. Taylor arrived yesterday in course, but owing to his being in the country did not receive it till this morning. The £200 enclosed, is I am confident a stretch of finance and I hope by studying economical measures will be adequate for my purposes, and trust in Providence will be the last I shall ever trouble my friends with. I am sorry I should have put you to the inconvenience of so many Postages, but as my matters have come so pressing I had scarcely leasure to call for a cover, and trust your goodness will forgive me. You mention you are to write me enclosing a proper plan of settlement through Mr. Dundas. This is a channel of conveyance I could have wished you to avoid, as Mr. Dundas though one of the best natured men in the world has put himself to a good deal of trouble on my account, and has promised to do more. I am unwilling to use such freedom with so great a man, and would more willingly have paid Postage. If you have not forwarded it already Captain Leith will enclose it under cover to Mr. Taylor through your last to which refer you. Have also wrote Mr. Luckie under cover to the Captain before I received his favor of the 14th inst. Give him my best respects, and I shall not fail to attend to any request coming from him.—Shall write him again when a little more at leasure a commodity of which I am very scarce at present having all my matters here to settle in a few days—so with love to you, Mr. Johnston, Mr. Luckie, etc. I remain

> Your affectionate Brother in haste

[*Addressed as under.*]   (signed) Robert Forbes.

London April nineteen 1800
> Mr. Forbes,
> > Mr. Robert Lamb, Merchant,

[*Franked.*]   Aberdeen.
H. Ferguson.

> 11, Fountain Court Strand,
> London,
> 26 April 1800.

My dear Sir

I was duly favoured with your kind letter of 16th inst., and return you and my friends my warmest acknowledgments four yor exertions in my entrest. To you my dear Sir who has advanced the means of prosecuting my wishes, I shall ever consider myself as deeply indebted for I am sensible that without your assistance there was no other Friend whom I could have looked up to for so great a favour, and I hope my future conduct shall be such that you will have no reason to think your favor misplaced. As this is probably the last time I shall have an opportunity of addressing you in Europe believe me I feel no small degree of satisfaction in adding that with regard to dangers and difficulties I am perfectly reconcilled—for though I am by no means addicted to superstition, yet I am authorized to say that in my opinion there has been a striking interposition of Providence in my favor, for what reason had I to expect the first interest in the Nation, for surely the favour of Mr. Dundas comes nothing short of that. And again the gradual steps by which I attained it is fully as noticeable—hear it. The first idea of it was suggested to me by our Friend Mr. Luckie.—He promised to speak to the Captain who had obtained some favour of this kind formerly the Captain writes his worthy friend Mr. Taylor. He applys to Mr. William Dundas Nephew to the Great Mr. Dundass one of his Majestys principal secretarys of state and President of all the India affairs in whose name I have been recommended to the India House and from whom I am in expectations of receiving letters of introduction to people in power at Madras which if I can obtain, Major Lacottie asured me yesterday will be worth twenty Comissions. This good fortune believe me has had a very striking effect on my mind which I believe will never be effaced, but make me more eager in pursuing the Friendly injunctions you have inculcated and trust by the assistance of the same Providence I shall be able to adhere to them. With regard to insuring my property I think there is little danger as we will start with a strong convoy, and besides each of the Indiamen carry from 35 to 40 Guns—and in our fleet there will be about 15 or 18. If convenient should be glad to hear from you before we sail address as before—Adieu my Dear Sir

Yours sincerely
(signed) Robert Forbes.

[Addressed to Mr. S. Johnston.]

L. Marischal College Diploma of M.A. granted to James Forbes, 3rd April, 1818.

OMNIBUS ET SINGULIS QUORUM INTEREST S.

Nos Gymnasiarcha et Artium et Linguarum Professores Moderatores Universitatis Marischallanae Abredonensis candide testamur probum et ingenuum adolescentem JACOBUM FORBES, filium legitimum Jacobi Forbes, Abredonensis, studiis Philosophicis Literisque humanioribus per quadriennium apud nos feliciter incubuisse, et post exactum studiorum curriculum ingenii sui ac eruditionis luculento specimine edito Gradum Magistri in Artibus liberalibus merito consecutum fuisse, quapropter eum omnibus bonorum morum et liberalium scientiarum fautoribus sedulo commendatum habemus ut eum humaniter amplecti ac benigne promovere dignentur: Quam gratiam oblata occasione libentissime referemus Nos qui chirographis nostris publicoque Universitatis sigillo Diploma hocce muniendum curavimus.

Datum Abredoniae tertio die Aprilis 〉 Anno Domini Millesimo octin- Geo. Glennie, S.S.T.D., Mor. P.P., gentesimo decimo octavo.   〉   Promotor.

Gul. Laur. Brown, S.S.T.D., et
  Gymnasiarcha.
Pat. Copland, LL.D., P.N.P.
Ro. Hamilton, LL.D., P.N.P.
Jno. Stuart, Lit. Gr. P.
Gul. Livingston, M.D., M.P.
Geo. French, M.D., Chem. P.
Jac. Kidd, LL.OO. P.
Ja. Davidson, M.D., H.N. et C. P.

Seal

M. Evidence led at the service of Sir Charles Forbes, Bart. of Newe, as heir male general of his great-great-grandfather, William Forbes, fifth of Newe, 12th March, 1830.*

"At Aberdeen the twelfth day of March 1830. In presence of the Jury impannelled by the Sheriff under a Claim of General Service presented by Sir Chas. Forbes of New and Edinglassie, Bart. as nearest and lawful Heir Male of William Forbes sometime of New his Great-Great-Grandfather: viz. :—

George Hogarth Junior Esq. Merchant Aberdeen
William Carnegie Esq. Advocate Aberdeen
James Milne Merchant there

* This evidence, which has been obtained through the courtesy of Dr. David Littlejohn, Sheriff Clerk of Aberdeenshire, is interesting as illustrating the method pursued in such services. It will be seen that Parish Registers are not even alluded to, and that no attempt is made to prove the extinction of the male issue of Alexander, second son of William Forbes, sixth of Newe.